MEETING
[GOD]
in
Scripture

Entering the

Psalms

MEETING
[GOD]
in
Scripture

Entering the
Psalms

LEADER'S
GUIDE

ANNE CRUMPLER

UPPER
ROOM BOOKS®
NASHVILLE

Library of Congress Cataloging-in-Publication Data

Crumpler, Anne B.
Entering the Psalms: leader's guide / Anne Crumpler.
    p. cm.— (Meeting God in Scripture series)
    Includes bibliographical references.
    ISBN 978-0-8358-9975-8
    1. Bible. O.T. Psalms—Study and teaching. I. Title.
    BS1430.55.C788 2009
    223'.2071—dc22   2008042916

Printed in the United States of America

Contents

Introduction

*W*elcome to *Meeting God in Scripture: Entering the Psalms.* For the next six weeks, you will be leading an exploration of the Psalms. This study of the Psalms builds on daily Bible readings (five per week) and personal exploration exercises (entry points) tied to the daily readings. The theme of the study is that worship, praying the psalms together, expresses our relationship to God and forms us in faith so that we begin to see ourselves and our lives in the context of God's love.

The daily Bible readings and responses require ten to fifteen minutes a day, and they lead up to and become the starting point for a weekly small-group meeting. This leader's guide includes a process and resources for an introductory meeting and eight weekly meetings of either 45 or 90 minutes. The time for the introductory meeting may vary, depending on how many persons attend and how many community-building activities you include.

Each element of the session has a suggested time frame for a group size of nine. A larger group will be unable to complete the activities in the suggested time. If you attempt to discuss in the whole group rather than in smaller groups of three, time will not allow completion of the activities. Therefore, we strongly encourage you to limit each group to no more than nine persons and to discuss in groups of three. For a larger group, you will need to reduce the time spent on each element or omit a portion from the session plan.

In the introductory meeting, you will present the approach, process, and content of the remaining sessions. (If your group has completed other studies in the Meeting God in Scripture series, the introductory session need not be repeated.) The primary difference between this resource and traditional Bible studies is its spiritual formation approach. To many participants, this approach may seem a dramatic departure from the analytical, left-brain methods that often characterize Bible study. Therefore, the introductory meeting will acquaint participants with the difference between formational and informational reading of the Bible. Meetings in the 90-minute format will include group *lectio divina* (contemplation of and individual response to scripture) in each session; the 45-minute format does *not* include group *lectio* each week. This accounts for the time difference between the two formats. Detailed directions for leading *lectio divina* follow this introduction. They will help you guide the group, and you may also use this information to create a computer presentation to aid your teaching.

At the back of this Leader's Guide you will find additional Psalm prayers from *The Upper Room Worshipbook: Music and Liturgies for Spiritual Formation* © 2006 Upper Room Books. Look for instructions within sessions 1, 2, 3, and 6 about how to enrich the sessions with the addition of these prayers.

Customizing the 90-minute Format for Your Group

The first 90-minute session includes get-acquainted activities, an introduction to *lectio divina*, and a group exploration of a scripture passage (EXPLORING THE WORD). Each session (after the introductory session) includes these components:

- Opening
- Interacting with the Word (in triads)
- Exploring the Word (group activity)
- Engaging the Word (*lectio divina*, 90-minute format only)
- Closing

At the end of this guide you will find a short introduction to the book of Psalms, written from a spiritual formation perspective. To prepare to lead each week, read the psalm you and participants will study that week. Reading the article "What Is Spiritual Formation?" (page 85) will ready you for the introductory session's exploration activity. Two additional articles, "Meeting God in Scripture" (page 91) and "Meeting God in Community" (page 101), will give you valuable background information as you lead this study.

Preparing the Meeting Space

The exercises in this study aim to involve participants on sensory and affective levels. A welcoming and worshipful atmosphere serves to reinforce those experiences. You may set up a worship center on a small table, using seasonal decorations that change weekly. Or you may develop a worship center with a Christ candle, a cross, and other symbols. A group member may have special gifts for creating such worship arrangements. During the introductory session, ask for volunteers who would prepare the worship center weekly.

Music adds greatly to the sessions. If you cannot lead singing, ask for a volunteer from the group to help with music/singing during opening and closing worship and prayer times. Compile a list of appropriate songs from the songbooks and hymnals available in your meeting place, and give these to the music leader before the first session. You may want to use the same hymn, chorus, or song to begin and end a session, so that you need to choose only six.

Each session will include conversation in groups of three about the week's readings and entry-point responses, so a setting in which chairs move easily from a circle arrangement (for OPENING and the large-group discussion of INTERACTING WITH THE WORD) into triads (for small-group discussion) would be advantageous.

When sessions include handouts, placing these on chairs or tables before participants arrive reduces confusion and creates a more peaceful atmosphere. If you plan to use a computer presentation, check it out before each session to reduce technological problems, confusion, and wasted time.

Looking Ahead: Supplies/Special Arrangements

All sessions: Participant's workbooks, newsprint or whiteboard and markers, extra Bibles, paper and writing utensils, name tags, candles, matches, hymnals, and a CD player and CDs (optional)

Intro session:	Words of the group agreement written on large sheets of paper, a picture of trees planted by a stream (hand drawn or downloaded from the Internet). Copies of "Obstacles to Hearing God in Scripture" (page 14) and "Informational and Formational Reading" (page 15) for each participant.
Session 1:	Large sheets of paper, newspapers, a variety of magazines, tape, markers, scissors, glue
Session 2:	Large sheets of paper, markers, copies of familiar music (optional)
Session 3:	Highlighters
Session 4:	Descriptions of people (written on slips of paper), basket
Session 5:	Large sheet of paper, marker, copies of questions, pens
Session 6:	Two copies of the Sunday newspaper, markers, notes on Psalm 46

Leading Lectio Divina in Groups (for 90-minute sessions)

Lectio divina is a Latin phrase often translated as "spiritual reading" or "holy reading." But for the first fifteen hundred years of the Christian church, people learned and absorbed the words and stories of scripture by *hearing* them read. Scrolls and books were rare, and most people could not read. Personal copies of the Bible in the language of ordinary life were not available until long after the invention of the printing press in the mid-1400s, and even then only to the wealthy. So when we hear scripture being read, we sit in company with the first saints who listened to hear God's personal word to them through the words of the Bible.

If you have never led *lectio divina* in a small group, the process outlined here may seem too simple to be effective. Please trust the approach. In just a few sessions you will see God at work as participants grow in their eagerness and ability to hear God speak to them through the words of scripture. Those who tested this resource emphasized that the group reflection on scripture was an invaluable part of the design. The time investment is worth the return for the participants. For more background on *lectio divina*, read "Meeting God in Scripture" (page 91).

Lectio divina is based on hearing a passage of scripture read several times. Using the directions below, you will guide group members in listening, reflecting in silence, talking with others, and praying in response to what they have heard. Allowing silence may be the most difficult part of the process for both leader and participants. Don't rush the silence; use a watch with a second hand to be sure you allow ample time for each step.

Preparing the Group to Listen

Before the first session of *lectio divina*, you may want to reflect together on "Obstacles to Hearing God in Scripture" (page 14) as group members think about all the things we do instead of listening—analyzing, classifying, and so on. The first two steps in the *lectio* process may be the most demanding because they require listening and silence. In the first step, you will invite group members to listen for a word or phrase from the Bible passage you read and to consider it in silence. The second tough step comes when you direct them to repeat *only* that word or phrase within their small group. They speak it aloud without comment or elaboration.

We are so accustomed to analyzing, to stepping back from scripture to *think about* what it means, that we often do not listen to the words themselves. For instance, if we read aloud the story of the persistent widow from Luke 18:1-8, some people will think and say within their group the word *perseverance*. But that word does not appear in the passage. That word and others like it (*compassion, mercy, faith*) are thoughts about the passage, and they reflect our analysis rather than the words we actually heard. Try to help group members realize that they are to listen for a word or phrase that occurs in the passage, not come up with a word to *describe* the passage. They are not to step back to analyze or categorize the reading.

Before you begin, invite group members to sit in groups of three, to become comfortable, and to prepare for a time of listening to scripture. Tell them that they will be hearing a passage of scripture—the same passage—read several times and that each reading will be followed by silence for reflection. Ask them to trust you to guide them through the process. Suggest that they give themselves fully to hearing the scripture—not reading along in their own Bibles but listening.

On the third reading, a group member will read the passage aloud so participants will hear it at least once in a voice other than yours. Ask for a volunteer to do this before beginning. Read the passage from the same translation each time to avoid distracting people by differences between the translations. You may want to photocopy from your Bible the page containing each session's *lectio divina* passage and mark the reading to make the change of readers less intrusive and to be sure the same translation is used. Tell the participants that the small groups will not be "reporting" to the entire body in any way and that what they say within their smaller groups will remain private.

The Process for Group *Lectio Divina*

STEP ONE: (first-stage reading) Tell group members that you will read the passage twice, once to orient them to its overall content and then again, more slowly, so that they can listen for a word or phrase that stops them or gets their attention. Read the passage aloud, twice.

In the silence, repeat your word or phrase to yourself and reflect on it.

Allow one to two minutes of silence. (*Time this step so you do not rush.*)

STEP TWO: **Within your group, repeat the word or phrase that attracted you—without comment, summary, or analysis. (Or you may pass.)**

STEP THREE: (second-stage reading) Ask group members to listen as you read the passage again, slowly, being open to how it connects to them. (Tell them that their word or phrase may or may not be the same one on this reading as during the first reading.)

In silence, consider how your word or phrase connects to your life right now—a situation, a feeling, a possibility.

Allow three minutes of silence for reflection.

STEP FOUR: (At this point, tell the group that participants may always choose not to speak by saying "pass" when their turn comes.)

In your groups, take a few minutes each to tell about the connection you sense between your life and your word or phrase. (Or you may pass.)

Ask the person closest to you in each group to be the first speaker.

STEP FIVE: (third-stage reading) Ask the alternate reader to read the passage again, slowly. Invite group members to listen during this reading for an invitation from God for the next few days.

In the silence, consider what invitation you hear from God. Be open to a sensory impression, an image, a song, a fragrance.

Allow three minutes of silence for reflection.

STEP SIX: Ask group members to ponder in silence the invitation they heard. Allow several minutes of silence.

STEP SEVEN: Invite each person to speak about the invitation he or she senses from God for his or her life in the next few days:

In your groups, allow each person to tell about the invitation he or she heard. (Or you may pass.)

This time, have the person farthest from you begin. This is an important step in the process, so allow ample time for each person to speak. Watch the groups; check to see which are finishing up, which need more time. Do not rush the process.

STEP EIGHT: Invite persons to pray for each other, one by one in turn, within their smaller groups. Ask each one to pray for the person to his or her right. The group members can decide whether they will pray aloud or silently.

Pray for each other to be empowered to respond to the invitations you heard. (You may pray silently or aloud.)

Remind participants to remain silent when their group finishes praying, since other groups may still be in prayer. When all have finished praying, say "amen" to end the process.[1]

You may want to debrief this experience of *lectio divina* by asking the group as a whole to comment on it: What worked for them? What was difficult about this way of responding to scripture? Have they been led through this process before, and, if so, what was different, better, or worse about it this time? This would be a good time to mention that everyone responds differently to the various ways of exploring scripture and that there is no expected outcome.

Obstacles to Hearing God in Scripture

Common obstacles:

- thinking/talking about scripture

- classifying

- comparing

- describing

- explaining

- looking for "the lesson" rather than listening to scripture:
the actual words that are there
the emotions we feel
the connections we make
the memories that arise

Permission is granted to make one copy for each participant.

Informational and Formational Reading

Reading for information is an integral part of teaching and learning. But reading is also concerned with listening for the special guidance, for the particular insight, for your relationship with God. What matters is the attitude of mind and heart.

Informational Reading

1. Informational reading is concerned with covering as much material as possible and as quickly as possible.

2. Informational reading is linear—seeking an objective meaning, truth, or principle to apply.

3. Informational reading seeks to master the text.

4. In informational reading, the text is an object out there for us to control.

5. Informational reading is analytical, critical, and judgmental.

6. Informational reading is concerned with problem solving.

Formational Reading

1. Formational reading is concerned with small portions of content rather than quantity.

2. Formational reading focuses on depth and seeks multiple layers of meaning in a single passage.

3. Formational reading allows the text to master the student.

4. Formational reading sees the student as the object to be shaped by the text.

5. Formational reading requires a humble, detached, willing, loving approach.

6. Formational reading is open to mystery. Students come to the scripture to stand before the Mystery called God and to let the Mystery address them.

Adapted from information in *Shaped by the Word: The Power of Scripture in Spiritual Formation*, rev. ed., by M. Robert Mulholland Jr. (Nashville, TN.: Upper Room Books, 2000), 49–63. Used by permission of Upper Room Books.

Introductory Session

Worship and Our Relationship to God

NOTE: If your group has used *Meeting God in Scripture* before, you may want to abbreviate the activities "Establishing a Group Agreement" and "Introducing Spiritual Formation as a Different Approach."

Preparing for the introductory session: Read the article "What Is Spiritual Formation?" (page 85, leader's guide) and the article "Reading Scripture Devotionally" (page 11, participant's workbook). Look over the chart comparing informational and formational approaches to reading scripture (page 15). Make copies of this chart to give to group members. If you plan to lead *lectio divina* in each session, be sure to provide copies of "Obstacles to Hearing God in Scripture" (page 14).

Note ideas from the articles that you feel are important. Read through the plan for the introductory session until you feel comfortable leading it, especially the readings from the Psalms and the reflection on them. You will need to tailor this session to fit your time frame. One place to save time might include passing out materials without a great deal of discussion.

Materials Needed

- Worship center (Christ candle, lighter or matches)
- Participant's workbooks. Since group members will be writing or drawing in their books as part of the daily reflection, each person will need his or her own copy.
- Name tags and markers
- The words *presence, prayer, preparation, participation, confidentiality,* and *courtesy* displayed on a large sheet of paper
- Extra Bibles for those who may not have brought theirs
- A picture of trees planted by a stream, hand drawn on a large sheet of paper or downloaded from the Internet
- Hymnals or CD player and CDs
- Copies (one for each participant) of "Informational and Formational Reading" (page 15) and "Obstacles to Hearing God in Scripture" (page 14)

Opening (5 minutes)

Welcome people as they arrive. Distribute the participant's workbooks as part of your greeting, and invite people to browse through the books until everyone arrives and the session begins. Ask everyone to wear a name tag.

Light the candle as a reminder of God's presence. Ask the participants to turn to page 19 in the participant's workbook and read together Psalm 145:1-3.

> I will extol you, my God and King,
>   and bless your name forever and ever.
> Every day I will bless you,
>   and praise your name forever and ever.
> Great is the LORD, and greatly to be praised;
>   his greatness is unsearchable.

Say a prayer:

God, you bring us together to praise your name. As we worship, bless us with your word and transform us in your amazing grace. Amen.

Establishing a Group Agreement (10 minutes)

Post a large sheet of paper on which you have written the words *presence, prayer, preparation, participation, confidentiality,* and *courtesy*. Explain what each means using the information below.

Presence: Attend each meeting unless serious reasons keep you away.

Prayer: Between meeting times, group members pray for one another and for the group's endeavors together.

Preparation: Group members make the daily readings and exercises a priority, doing them as diligently as life allows.

Participation: Group members will participate honestly and openly in the activities of the sessions.

Confidentiality: What is said within the group remains in the group. Members will not discuss outside the group anything others say within this setting.

Courtesy: Group members will listen to one another with respect and without interrupting or engaging in side conversations. When opinions differ, group members will not attempt to persuade anyone to any point of view but will listen for what God may be saying in the differences.

Ask the participants if they want to accept, add to, or modify the group agreement. Plan to display the agreement each time the group meets.

Introducing Spiritual Formation as a Different Approach (20 minutes)

Explain that this study of the Bible will probably differ from other studies the group has participated in. Distribute copies of the chart "Informational and Formational Reading" (page 15, leader's guide), which compares two ways of reading the Bible and other Christian resources. Talk about the entries on the chart and help group members to compare the two approaches. Point out that our educational system concentrates on helping students develop left-brain, analytical skills and often presents education as a linear process focusing on cognitive abilities. As an example, ask participants to think about the difference between art classes and math classes in a secular learning setting or about a quantifying (grades, reports, assessments) rather than a relational focus in education. Tell the group members that they will be approaching scripture as an opportunity to encounter God and to learn about themselves and one another.

Invite people to open their workbooks to the Introductory Session, page 19, and to read "How Long?" the entry point for Psalm 6:6-8, and "The Heart's Examination," the entry point for Psalm 15:1-5. Ask, **How do these activities differ from ways you have studied the Bible before?** List the group's responses on a large sheet of paper.

Direct the participants to the article "Reading Scripture Devotionally" (page 11, participant's workbook), and give them time to read the article. Then ask the group members to compare the article's ideas to their responses listed on the large sheet of paper. In what ways do their ideas echo the article? How do their ideas differ from those in the article?

Explain that the ideas in the article shape this study. If people have questions or concerns raised by the article, respond to them or ask others in the group to respond.

Each day the participants will read a psalm. Then they will read again, looking more closely at one verse or a few verses from the psalm. They will respond to the verse or verses by following the process suggested in the entry point. Each day's reading and activity will take about ten or fifteen minutes to complete.

The "starred" entry point: One of each week's entry points has two stars beside the title. Invite the group to look at the starred article on page 32. Urge the participants to make time to do the starred activity each week even if they are too busy to do them all. The starred activity will be part of the weekly group meeting.

Direct their attention to the section of the introduction titled "If You Want to Do More: Keeping a Spiritual Journal" (page 8) and talk about keeping a journal. Ask if any in the group have kept a journal. If so, invite these persons to tell the group the benefits they received from the practice. Emphasize that journals are private, and no one will be asked to reveal anything he or she has written.

Exploring the Word (15 minutes)

Ask someone to read aloud Psalm1:3, which describes people of faith.

> They are like trees
>   planted by streams of water,
> which yield their fruit in its season
>   and their leaves do not wither.

Display a picture of trees in full bloom, planted by a stream, their roots reaching into the land and water.

Invite people to work with partners they do not know well. Allow a few minutes for introductions. Give one person in each pair a marker. Ask the other person in each pair to answer these questions:

- What is one prayer, scripture, hymn, or part of the worship service that grounds your faith?
- What is one way that your faith affects the way you live day to day?

Tell the person with the marker to write his or her partner's responses on the roots and on the branches of the trees in the picture. Then ask the partners to change places.

Bring the group together to reflect on the picture.

Invite people to describe other spiritual formation images drawn from the psalm. They may want to complete the sentence, "Spiritual formation is like . . ." ("Spiritual formation is like being planted, watered, and nourished in faith.") Or they may prefer to describe some of the ways we are formed in faith: "Saying prayers, singing hymns, and listening to God's word nourish us in faith." "Faith grounds us as we branch out into the world." Write the group's responses on the picture.

Conclude the activity by inviting the group to read together Psalm 1:1-3.

Closing (5 minutes)

Invite the group members to sing together hymns that have helped to form their faith.

To conclude the session, ask the group to read aloud together Psalm 145:1-3 (page 19, participant's workbook).

Extinguish the candle.

Ask for volunteers who might be willing to assist in music selection and singing or those who might enjoy helping set up the worship center each week.

Preparing for Session 1

- Complete the daily readings and entry-point exercises in the participant's workbook.

- Read the introduction to Psalms (page 67).

- Read "The Theme of This Study" (page 8, participant's workbook).

- Review the pattern for leading *lectio divina* (pages 12–13, leader's guide) until you feel comfortable using it; photocopy and mark the passage for the alternate reader.

- Prepare materials for the worship center.

- Have available materials for EXPLORING THE WORD: large sheets of paper (such as newsprint), newspapers, a variety of magazines, markers, and tape, scissors, glue, copies of Psalm prayers for Session 1 (pages 77–78, leader's guide). Post or make copies of Psalm 147 for the CLOSING.

Let no day
pass by without reading
some portion of the

Sacred Scriptures
and giving some space to

meditation;
for nothing feeds the soul
so well as those sacred studies do.

THEONAS OF ALEXANDRIA (C. 300)

The Epistle of Theonas

Psalms of

Praise

NOTE: All meeting outlines are for 90-minute sessions; if you are using this study in a 45-minute session, you will need to abbreviate and adapt the opening and closing prayers and omit the *lectio divina* experience.

Have name tags and markers available every week.

Opening (5 minutes)

Light the candle as a reminder of God's presence.

Invite a group member to read aloud Psalm 147:1:

> Praise the LORD!
> How good it is to sing praises to our God;
>   for he is gracious, and a song of praise is fitting.

Encourage the group to sing a hymn of praise such as "Holy God, We Praise Thy Name" (verses 1 and 3) or "Joyful, Joyful, We Adore Thee."

Say a prayer:

We praise you, God, for creating and sustaining the heavens and earth, the world and all that lives in it, and for guiding us through each day of our lives. Give us awe in your presence and words to praise your holy name. Amen.

Introduce the study *Meeting God in Scripture: Entering the Psalms.* Give people a few minutes to read "The Theme of This Study: Worship and Our Relationship to God" (page 8, participant's workbook). Then say, **Psalms are the hymns and prayers of worship that express our relationship with God.**

Interacting with the Word (15 minutes)

Begin by allowing participants a couple of minutes to review their comments and daily responses to the Bible readings in their participant's workbook.

Below are several questions the smaller groups (triads) might use when discussing each week's Bible reading and responses. Choose two of the questions for discussion this week and gauge the group's response to them. You may use the same questions each week or vary them. Write the questions you'll be using on a board or flip chart.

Encourage group members to listen for God in each person's words, allowing each participant time to respond to a question before the group moves on to the next.

Some possible questions:

- What scripture reading and accompanying entry point drew the most response from you?
- What scripture reading and entry-point activity most surprised you?
- What did you learn through the week's readings?
- What insight did you connect with your life?
- What persons or ideas touched on this week would you like to know more about?
- What reading most challenged you?
- What questions do you have about the week's readings?
- What relationships do you see differently due to the week's readings and responses?
- How did your actions or attitudes change in response to the daily Bible readings?

If you prefer, use questions of your own.

Exploring the Word (20 minutes)

This activity builds on the entry point for Psalm 147 (day 5).

Say, **The psalms for this week are hymns of praise that express adoration of God, who is both Creator and Savior. God creates the world, redeems it, and sustains it in an ongoing process. The God of the majestic mountains and roaring seas is also the God of humankind: the people of God, the societies and nations of the human world, each individual person.**

Write each of the following at the top a large sheet of paper:

"God Creates and Sustains the Universe"

"God Saves the People of God"

"God Is the Lord of Nations"

"God Loves Each Person"

Invite people to make collages praising God. Explain that these large sheets will be posted around the room (on the wall or spread out on a table). Ask persons to visit each sheet three times, each time reading Psalm 147 and adding a new dimension to the collage. You may want to post the following brief directions at each sheet of paper, along with scissors, glue, magazines and newspapers, Bibles, and markers.

First, prayerfully consider what the psalm says about God's activity in the world. Write brief paraphrases of the psalm that describe aspects of God's activity. Refer to some of the photocopied psalm prayers that are lying next to the posted sheets of paper.

Second, using the newspapers and magazines, add pictures and articles that describe God's activity in the natural and human world to the collages.

Third, write brief descriptions or draw pictures of God's activity in your own life.

Finally, invite the participants to walk around the room looking at the collages and reflecting in silence on all that God has done. Bring the group together. Ask each person, in turn, to say a sentence prayer expressing praise for one aspect of God's activity in the world.

Conclude the activity by inviting the group to pray together Psalm 147.

Engaging the Word (lectio divina, 45 minutes)

Use the steps outlined for leading group *lectio divina* to guide the group through contemplation of **Psalm 150.** (See pages 12–13, leader's guide.)

As a concluding step, invite the group to say together Psalm 150.

Closing (5 minutes)

Ask each person to reflect in silence, considering these questions:

• How has your faith been influenced by praising God?

• In what way does praise affect the way you live?

• What would it mean, this coming week, to live your daily life always praising God?

Encourage the group members to sing together a hymn of praise.

Invite the group to say together Psalm 147:1:

> Praise the LORD!
> How good it is to sing praises to our God;
>   for he is gracious, and a song of praise is fitting.

Conclude with a benediction: **May God bless you with wonder at all God's good gifts, so that you will live every day praising the Lord.**

Extinguish the candle.

Preparing for Session 2

• Complete the daily readings and entry-point activities in the participant's workbook.

• Review the pattern for leading *lectio divina,* and photocopy and mark the passage for the alternate reader.

• Prepare materials for the worship center and EXPLORING THE WORD: large pieces of paper, markers, Bibles of the same version for everyone, questions for activity prewritten on newsprint.

• Post Psalm 22:2-4, 19 for OPENING.

Scripture
is like a river,
broad and deep,
shallow enough here
for the lamb to go wading,
but deep enough there
for the elephant to swim.

GREGORY THE GREAT (C. 540-604)

Moralia in Iob, Book I

Psalms of

Petition

NOTE: All meeting outlines are for 90-minute sessions; if you are using this study in a 45-minute session, you will need to abbreviate and adapt the opening and closing prayers and omit the *lectio divina* experience.

Have name tags and markers available every week.

Opening (5 minutes)

Light the candle as a reminder of God's presence.

Invite the group to say together Psalm 22:2-4, 19:

> O my God, I cry by day, but you do not answer;
>   and by night, but find no rest.
> Yet you are holy,
>   enthroned on the praises of Israel.
> In you our ancestors trusted;
>   they trusted, and you delivered them.
>
> . . . .

> But you, O Lord, do not be far away!
>> O my help, come quickly to my aid!

Encourage the group to sing a hymn of strength in tribulation, such as "Come, Ye Disconsolate"; "Out of the Depths I Cry to You"; or "How Firm a Foundation."

Review the overall theme of the study *Meeting God in Scripture: Entering the Psalms.* Say, **Psalms are the hymns and prayers of worship that express our relationship to God.**

Say a prayer:

Hear our prayers, O Lord, and help us in times of trouble. Give us faith to put our lives in your hands, trusting in your promises and finding hope in your amazing grace. Amen.

Interacting with the Word (15 minutes)

Allow a few minutes for silent reflection as people review the week's scripture readings and entry points as well as the comments and responses they have written in their participant's workbooks.

Invite the participants to form small groups of two or three people to discuss the week's Bible readings and responses. Ask the groups to discuss the same questions they used last week, choose others from the list, or create new questions. Write the questions on a large sheet of paper. Encourage group members to listen for God in each person's words and to give everyone time to respond to a question before moving on to the next.

Bring the groups together. Invite people to report on their discussions:

- In what ways were your responses to the readings similar? How were they different?
- What did you learn about the Psalms?
- What one word would you use to describe the psalms you read this week?

Exploring the Word (20 minutes)

This activity builds on the entry point for Psalm 12 (day 4).

Say, **This week's scripture readings are petitionary psalms: individual and community laments. The people bring human suffering before God and pray for help. Laments describe fear, distress, anger, loneliness, violence, confusion, indignation, wounded hearts, and broken bodies—the depths of suffering. The psalmists bring their laments** to God because they trust in God's concern and faithfulness. God's steadfast love offers hope for all generations.

Be sure everyone has a Bible of the same version. Invite the group to read aloud Psalm 12.

Tell people to form two groups. Give each group a large sheet of paper and a marker. Explain that one group will write two or three stanzas of a community lament, based on Psalm 12; the other group will write a refrain that will be added to the lament.

Invite the members of one group to talk about Psalm 12, using these questions to guide their discussion:

- What evidence of corruption do you see in your community?
- In what ways has truth succumbed to flattery, boasting, lies, and doublespeak?
- How are the poor and needy treated?
- In what areas of your community is "vileness . . . exalted"?
- What sense do you have that "the faithful have disappeared from humankind"?

Ask one group to write two or three stanzas of a community lament, using contemporary examples. Invite one person in the group to record the lament on a large sheet of paper.

Invite the members of the other group to talk about Psalm 12, using these questions and scripture passages to guide their discussion:

- What does God promise? (Read Isaiah 25:6-10; 32:1-8, 16-18.)
- What does God promise for the poor and needy? (Read Isaiah 41:17; 61:1.)
- How does God promise to change human communities?
- When have you seen God at work in your community to bring about God's promised salvation?

Ask this group to write a refrain, expressing trust in God's promises and calling on God to intervene in the community to bring about change. Invite one person in the group to record the refrain on a large sheet of paper.

Bring the groups together to read responsively the psalm they have written, alternating a stanza with the refrain.

OPTIONAL: If you have time, invite the group to set the psalm to music. Encourage the participants to create a melody that fits the rhythm and words. Or provide a tune, such as Tallis' Canon or Old One-Hundredth, and suggest they write words that fit the music.

Engaging the Word (lectio divina, 45 minutes)

Use the steps outlined for leading group *lectio* to guide the group through contemplation of **Psalm 130**. (See pages 12–13, leader's guide.)

As a concluding step, invite the group to say together Psalm 130 or read to the group the Psalm prayer found on page 79 of this guide.

Closing (5 minutes)

Ask each person to reflect in silence, considering these questions:

- When have you experienced God in the midst of your grief or suffering?
- How has this experience changed your faith or relationship with God?
- Where in your life do you need to rely on the trust and comfort you learned in that time?

Invite the group members to sing together a hymn of strength in tribulation.

Ask one group member to say aloud Psalm 51:12:

> Restore to me the joy of your salvation,
>   and sustain in me a willing spirit.

Conclude with a benediction: **May God bless you with faith in God's promises, so that you may live at peace even in times of affliction.**

Extinguish the candle.

Preparing for Session 3

- Complete the daily readings and entry-point responses in the participant's workbook.
- Review the pattern for leading *lectio divina*, and photocopy and mark the passage for the alternate reader.
- Prepare materials for the worship center.
- Copy of Psalm 84:1-2 to post for OPENING.
- Practice reading the guided meditation for EXPLORING THE WORD.

Even when carrying out needful tasks, keep meditating inwardly and praying. Thus you can grasp the depths of divine Scripture and the power hidden in it, and "pray without ceasing."

ABBA PHILIMON (LATE SIXTH CENTURY?)

The Philokalia (Volume Two)

Psalms of

Pilgrimage

NOTE: All meeting outlines are for 90-minute sessions; if you are using this study in a 45-minute session, you will need to abbreviate and adapt the opening and closing prayers and omit the *lectio divina* experience.

Have name tags and markers available every week.

Opening (5 minutes)

Light the candle as a reminder of God's presence.

Invite the group to say together Psalm 84:1-2:

> How lovely is your dwelling place,
>   O LORD of hosts!
> My soul longs, indeed it faints
>   for the courts of the LORD;
> My heart and my flesh sing for joy
>   to the living God.

Encourage the group to sing a hymn such as "Come, We that Love the Lord" or "Arise, Shine Out, Your Light Has Come."

Say a prayer:

God, we come into your presence with joy, knowing that you are always gracious and welcome us with love. Amen.

Review the overall theme of the study *Meeting God in Scripture: Entering the Psalms*, saying, **Psalms are the hymns and prayers of worship that express our relationship to God.**

Invite the group to sing together the closing verses of the chosen hymn.

Interacting with the Word (15 minutes)

Allow a few minutes for silent reflection as people review the week's scripture readings and entry points as well as the comments and responses they have written in their participant's workbooks.

Invite the participants to form small groups of two or three people to discuss the week's Bible readings and activities. Ask the groups to discuss the same questions they used last week, choose others from the list, or create new questions. Write the questions on a large sheet of paper. Encourage group members to listen for God in each person's words and to give everyone time to respond to a question before moving on to the next.

Bring the groups together. Invite people to report on their discussions:

- In what ways were your responses to the readings similar? How were they different?
- What did you learn about the Psalms?
- What one word would you use to describe the psalms you read this week?

Exploring the Word (20 minutes)

This activity builds on the entry point for Psalm 122 (day 3).

Say, **The scripture readings for this week are pilgrim and processional psalms, celebrating Jerusalem, the Temple sanctuary, and entry into the presence of the Lord.**

Invite the group to read aloud Psalm 122, or read aloud to them one of the psalm prayers found on page 80 of this guide.

Explain that the psalm is layered. One layer describes a pilgrimage to Jerusalem. A second layer recalls the history and rituals of the people of God. A third layer draws on hopes for a messiah and for "the new Jerusalem," when all nations will come together in peace. The word *Jerusalem* means "city of peace."

Ask people to write in their workbooks the words of Psalm 122 that

- refer to a pilgrimage to Jerusalem.
- recall the history and rituals of the people of God.
- draw on hope for a new Jerusalem when all nations will come together in peace.

Invite the group to participate in a guided meditation. Ask people to find places in the room where they can be alone and quiet. Invite them to get comfortable, to close their eyes, and to listen to their breathing as they relax and begin to focus on the sound of your voice.

Read the following guided meditation. Read slowly, pausing after each sentence. Allow times of silence so individuals may follow their personal reflection.

PILGRIMAGE TO JERUSALEM: A GUIDED MEDITATION

As you close your eyes, slow your breathing and relax your body; prepare yourself for a journey back in time to the city of Jerusalem, the city of peace. . . .

When you are ready, open your mind's eye to see the land, the land where Abraham walked, where God stood with him, saying, "To you and your children, I will give this land." Think of Moses leading the people out of Egypt and across the wilderness to Mount Sinai where the Hebrews received God's law. Remember Joshua leading the people across the Jordan into the Promised Land, where they grew and prospered and became a nation.

See in your mind's eye Jerusalem, the city of David, Solomon, Isaiah, and Jesus. *(Allow one or two minutes for silent reflection.)*

Walk the winding streets through the old city; touch the adobe walls; hear the merchants in the market; see the colors: red rugs, purple cloth, earthenware jugs, bowls of orange spice, pomegranates, grapes. Join the crush of people crowding city streets.

Walk to the Temple Mount, built high over the city, drawing pilgrims from east, west, north, and south to worship—all the people of God singing in glad celebration "to give thanks to the name of the LORD." Imagine the Holy of Holies where the high priest prays and the presence of God spreads out in golden glory.

Now imagine the same scene from high above the city. See the shoreline, the rocky cliffs, the rivers, the desert sand. Choose a road below and follow it into the present-day city of Jerusalem. When your feet are standing within the gates of the city, stop and look around. (*Allow one or two minutes for silent reflection.*)

On a street corner, a soldier stands alert. Another leans against a crumbling wall, cradling a rifle amid religious shrines and signs of war. Hateful words are scrawled on adobe walls, and tanks roll down streets where prophets spoke.

"Pray for the peace of Jerusalem." Pray for the peace of the world. (*Allow several minutes for silent prayer.*)

Tell people to open their eyes and return to the group when they are ready.

Invite one group member to pray aloud Psalm 122.

Engaging the Word (lectio divina, 45 minutes)

Use the steps outlined for leading group *lectio divina* to guide the group through contemplation of **Psalm 100**. (See pages 12–13, leader's guide.)

As a concluding step, invite the group to say responsively Psalm 100, or read aloud to them one of the psalm prayers found on page 81 of this guide.

Closing (5 minutes)

Ask each person to reflect in silence, considering these questions:

- In what ways do you travel each day with God?
- How might the perspective of pilgrimage affect the way you live out your discipleship?
- What would it mean, this coming week, to live as a pilgrim?

Invite the group members to sing together a hymn celebrating God's presence.

Encourage the group to say together Psalm 84:3*b*-4:

> O LORD of hosts,
>   my King and my God.
> Happy are those who live in your house,
>   ever singing your praise.

Conclude with a benediction: **Peace be among you. God's peace be with you.**

Extinguish the candle.

Preparing for Session 4

- Complete the daily readings and entry-point activities in the participant's workbook.
- Review the pattern for leading *lectio divina*, and photocopy and mark the passage for the alternate reader.
- Prepare materials for the worship center.
- Prepare descriptions for EXPLORING THE WORD. Either write the descriptions on slips of paper or photocopy the page and cut them apart. Put the slips of paper in a basket.
- Copy of Psalm 72:18-19 to post for CLOSING.

Reading

seeks for the sweetness
of a blessed life,
meditation perceives it,
prayer asks for it,
contemplation tastes it.

GUIGO II (D. 1188)

The Ladder of Monks

Psalms of

Royalty

NOTE: All meeting outlines are for 90-minute sessions; if you are using this study in a 45-minute session, you will need to abbreviate and adapt the opening and closing prayers and omit the *lectio divina* experience.

Have name tags and markers available every week.

Opening (5 minutes)

Light the candle as a reminder of God's presence.

Invite one group member to say aloud Psalm 18:1-3*a*.

> I love you, O LORD, my strength.
> The LORD is my rock, my fortress, and my deliverer,
>   my God, my rock in whom I take refuge,
>   my shield, and the horn of my salvation, my stronghold.
> I call upon the LORD, who is worthy to be praised.

Encourage the group to sing a hymn of God's rule such as "O Worship the King" or "Praise, My Soul, the King of Heaven."

Review the overall theme of the study *Meeting God in Scripture: Entering the Psalms,* saying, **Psalms are the hymns and prayers of worship that express our relationship to God.**

Say a prayer:

God, give us faith to honor your authority, insight to understand your purpose, and courage to do your will. Amen.

Interacting with the Word (15 minutes)

Allow a few minutes for silent reflection as people review the week's scripture readings and entry points as well as the comments and responses they have written in their participant's workbooks.

Invite the participants to form small groups of two or three people to discuss the week's Bible readings and activities. Ask the groups to discuss the same questions they used last week, choose others from the list, or create new questions. Write the questions on a large sheet of paper. Encourage group members to listen for God in each person's words and to give everyone time to respond to a question before moving on to the next.

Bring the groups together. Invite people to report on their discussions:

- In what ways were your responses to the readings similar? How were they different?
- What did you learn about the Psalms?
- What one word would you use to describe the psalms you read this week?

Exploring the Word (20 minutes)

This activity builds on the entry point for Psalm 96 (day 4).

Say, **This week's scripture readings are royal psalms that ask God's blessings on the king; praise kings who rule with justice, righteousness, and mercy; and look forward to the reign of the messianic king. They all assume that God is the ultimate authority, the king of kings and the lord of all creation.**

Invite the group members to turn in their Bibles and read Psalm 96.

Explain: **Psalm 96 announces the coming of God's kingdom, in which the purposes of God—peace, justice, equity, righteousness, life, mercy, health, generosity, abundance, love—will be fulfilled, and God's universal rule will be established once and for all. God is coming to rule the earth with righteousness and truth. Psalm 96 is a call to proclaim God's reign. We are to be like trumpets announcing the king's arrival.**

Write on slips of paper the following descriptions or copy this page and cut them into strips. (Feel free to make changes or additions that relate to the particular circumstances of your group.) Put the slips of paper in a basket.

- a coworker who grew up in the church but whose faith has lapsed: "I still believe in God—I guess."

- a friend who is thinking of leaving the church you both attend: "If there's a God, how come the world is falling apart? Every time I see the news, someone else is being murdered or a hurricane has blown away another city. Why does God let it happen?—if there is a God."

- a young man your church has helped to settle in this country. He practices Buddhism. (Buddha preached a religion without authority, ritual, tradition, or theology. Buddhism says that life is suffering, caused by desire for private fulfillment. Overcoming desire, through disciplined thought and behavior, is the path to nirvana, the ultimate destiny of the human spirit.)

- a committee of your city council voting on legislation that will encourage socioeconomic diversity and will require every neighborhood or apartment complex to include a percentage of low-income housing.

- a mother whose child has been diagnosed with childhood leukemia.

- your church board, which is struggling to decide what to keep and what to cut in the proposed budget for next year.

- a homeless teenager who sleeps next to the side door of your church.

- an artist in your community who is planning a trip to Arizona to paint California condors, the largest birds in the world and an endangered species. A member of your church wants to collect an offering to contribute to her trip.

- a group of children sponsoring a recycle-reuse program in your community.

Invite people to form small groups. Ask a representative from each group to draw two slips of paper from the basket. Then invite the members of each group to discuss:

- In what ways does God's promised kingdom relate to the situation of the person or people described on the slip of paper?

- How would you proclaim God's reign to the person or people described?
- What form of communication would you use?
- What would you say?
- How would your actions speak for God's rule, and how would you explain your actions?

Bring the groups together. Ask each group either to tell or to present how it would proclaim that God is king.

Conclude the activity by inviting the group members to pray together Psalm 46 or read aloud to them one of the Psalm prayers found on page 79 of this guide.

Engaging the Word (lectio divina, 45 minutes)

Use the steps outlined for leading group *lectio divina* to guide the group through contemplation of **Psalm 47**. (See pages 12–13, leader's guide.)

As a concluding step, invite the group to say together Psalm 47.

Closing (5 minutes)

Ask each person to reflect in silence, considering these questions:

- In which areas of your life do you worship God as king? In which areas do you worship another god? What areas do you keep from God?
- What does the kingship of God mean for you in your daily living?
- What would it mean, this coming week, to live your daily life serving God as king?

Invite the group members to sing together a hymn celebrating God's rule.

Invite the group to say together Psalm 72:18-19.

> Blessed be the LORD, the God of Israel,
>   who alone does wondrous things.
> Blessed be his glorious name forever;
>   may his glory fill the whole earth.
>   Amen and Amen.

Conclude with a benediction: **The Lord is king of all the earth. May you sing, each day, a new song to the Lord.**

Extinguish the candle.

Preparing for Session 5

- Complete the daily readings and entry-point activities in the participant's workbook.

- Review the pattern for leading *lectio divina*, and photocopy and mark the passage for the alternate reader.

- Copies of the opening psalm verses, to be read responsively

- Prepare materials for the worship center and EXPLORING THE WORD: a copy of the questions for Psalm 73 (page 57) for each participant and pens or pencils

- Copy of Psalm 73:28 to post for CLOSING.

If God's word is so
full of consolations,
what overflowing
springs shall we find in
God himself?
If the promise is so
sweet, what will the
performance be?

RICHARD BAXTER (1615-1691)

The Saints' Everlasting Rest

Psalms of

Wisdom

NOTE: All meeting outlines are for 90-minute sessions; if you are using this study in a 45-minute session, you will need to abbreviate and adapt the opening and closing prayers and omit the *lectio divina* experience.

Have name tags and markers available every week.

Opening (5 minutes)

Light the candle as a reminder of God's presence.

Invite two participants to say responsively Psalm 37:3-4, 23-24:

> Trust in the LORD, and do good;
>> so you will live in the land, and enjoy security.
> Take delight in the LORD,
>> and he will give you the desires of your heart.
>
> . . . .
>
> Our steps are made firm by the LORD,
>> when he delights in our way;

> Though we stumble, we shall not fall headlong,
>   for the LORD holds us by the hand.

Encourage the group to sing a hymn such as "Immortal, Invisible, God Only Wise"; "Give to the Winds Thy Fears"; or "Thy Holy Wings, O Savior" (verse 1).

Review the overall theme of the study *Meeting God in Scripture: Entering the Psalms,* saying, **Psalms are the hymns and prayers of worship that express our relationship to God.**

Say a prayer:

God, draw us near to you and teach us your ways so that we may live in obedience, according to your purposes. Amen.

Interacting with the Word (15 minutes)

Allow a few minutes for silent reflection as people review the week's scripture readings and entry points as well as the comments and responses they have written in their participant's workbooks.

Invite the participants to form small groups of two or three people to discuss the week's Bible readings and activities. Ask the groups to discuss the same questions they used last week, choose others from the list, or create new questions. Write the questions on a large sheet of paper. Encourage group members to listen for God in each person's words and to give everyone time to respond to a question before moving on to the next.

Bring the groups together. Invite people to report on their discussions:

• In what ways were your responses to the readings similar? How were they different?

• What did you learn about the Psalms?

• What one word would you use to describe the psalms you read this week?

Exploring the Word (20 minutes)

This activity builds on the entry point for Psalm 73 (day 3).

Say, **This week's scripture readings are Wisdom Psalms. Wisdom, in the Bible, means skill, common sense, book learning, courtesy, morality, and reverence for God. It also refers to the ways of God revealed in creation and in the daily lives of human beings.**

Psalm 73 describes a transformation in the psalmist's faith from pat answers to skepticism to reliance on God and evangelism.

Give each participant a copy of the questions for Psalm 73 (page 57) and a pen or pencil. Ask participants to reflect on the sets of questions and to note their responses.

When everyone has had time to answer the questions, ask the participants to turn the paper over and write "The Road of Faith" at the top of the paper. Ask them to draw a long road that represents the psalmist's journey, marking five points on the road that represent the changes in his journey.

Next, ask participants to draw their own Road of Faith. How is it similar and different from the psalmist's? Where do the paths overlap or diverge?

Have persons form groups of two or three to share their drawings and reflections.

Bring the group together. Conclude the activity by inviting a group member to pray aloud Psalm 73 .

Engaging the Word (lectio divina, 45 minutes)

Use the steps outlined for leading group *lectio divina* to guide the group through contemplation of **Psalm 111**. (See pages 12–13, leader's guide.)

As a concluding step, invite the group to say together Psalm 111.

Closing (5 minutes)

Ask each person to reflect in silence, considering these questions:

- Where in your journey have you received or displayed the most wisdom? Are these places and situations the same or different?
- How does choosing to follow the wisdom of God affect the way you live?
- What would it mean, this coming week, to live your daily life following God's guidance?

Invite the group members to sing together a hymn of trust in God's wisdom.

Invite the group to say together Psalm 73:28.

> But for me it is good to be near God;
> I have made the Lord God my refuge,
> to tell of all your works.

Conclude with a benediction: **May God bring you close and guide your life day to day.**
Extinguish the candle

Preparing for Session 6

- Complete the daily readings and entry-point activities in the participant's workbook.

- Review the pattern for leading *lectio divina*, and photocopy and mark the passage for the alternate reader.

- Prepare materials for the worship center.

- For EXPLORING THE WORD, you will need two copies of the Sunday newspaper, markers, Bibles, paper, pens, "Notes on Psalm 46" (page 65, one per participant)

Psalm 73

1

What does the psalmist believe at first (verse 1)?

How is the psalmist's belief commonly stated today? Do you agree? disagree?

What other beliefs are popular in the church today?

2

What made the psalmist question his or her belief (verses 2-14)?

What questions do you have about your faith?

What about the world today leads you to question your beliefs in and about God?

3

What brought about the transformation in the psalmist's faith (verses 16-20)?

How does worship in the community influence your faith?

What helps you to resolve your questions about God?

4

How does the psalmist describe the transformation (verses 21-26)?

What does the psalmist discover about his or her relationship to God?

How has your relationship to God changed? What has not changed?

How would you describe your relationship to God now?

5

Once the psalmist comes to terms with his or her faith, what does the psalmist do (verse 28)?

What does it mean for you to take refuge in the Lord?

When have you told other people about God? What have you told them?

Permission is granted to make one copy for each participant.

We pray

to see life as it is,
to *understand* it, and to
make it *better* than it was.
We pray so that reality
can break into our *souls*
and give us back our
awareness of the
Divine Presence in *life*.

JOAN CHITTISTER, O.S.B.

Wisdom Distilled from the Daily (1991)

Psalms of

Faith and Trust

NOTE: All meeting outlines are for 90-minute sessions; if you are using this study in a 45-minute session, you will need to abbreviate and adapt the opening and closing prayers and omit the *lectio divina* experience.

Have name tags and markers available every week.

Opening (5 minutes)

Light the candle as a reminder of God's presence.

Invite the group to say together Psalm 16:8, 11 or read aloud the Psalm prayer on page 82 of this guide.

> I keep the LORD always before me;
> > because he is at my right hand, I shall not be moved. . . .
>
> You show me the path of life.
> > In your presence there is fullness of joy;
> > in your right hand are pleasures forevermore.

Encourage the group to sing a hymn of faith: "A Mighty Fortress Is Our God."

Review the overall theme of the study *Meeting God in Scripture: Entering the Psalms*, saying, **Psalms are the hymns and prayers of worship that express our relationship to God.**

Say a prayer:

Thank you, God, for faith that relies on you to still a stormy world and to establish a new creation in your love. Amen.

Interacting with the Word (15 minutes)

Allow a few minutes for silent reflection as people review the week's scripture readings and entry points as well as the comments and responses they have written in their participant's workbooks.

Invite the participants to form small groups of two or three people to discuss the week's Bible readings and activities. Ask the groups to discuss the same questions they used last week, choose others from the list, or create new questions. Write the questions on a large sheet of paper. Encourage group members to listen for God in each person's words and to give everyone time to respond to a question before moving on to the next.

Bring the groups together. Invite people to report on their discussions:

* In what ways were your responses to the readings similar? How were they different?
* What did you learn about the Psalms?
* What one word would you use to describe the psalms you read this week?

Exploring the Word (20 minutes)

This activity builds on the entry point for Psalm 46 (day 3).

Say, **The psalms for this week describe our relationship to God. God is our refuge, delight, joy. We long for God and are satisfied. These psalms describe faith, trust, certainty, security in the Lord, who is present in all the circumstances of our lives.**

Have available two copies of the Sunday newspaper. Invite people to read the paper, taking note of articles about natural disaster, war, national and international turmoil, and articles that might contribute to the frightened, frantic busyness of our lives.

Post sheets of the newspaper on a wall. Write on them "Be still, and know that I am God!"

Give each person a Bible, two or three sheets of paper, a pen, and a copy of "Notes on Psalm

46" (page 65, leader's guide). Ask individuals to find places in the room where they can be alone and quiet. Encourage participants to read Psalm 46 and the notes on the psalm.

After a few minutes of silent reflection, invite each person to write an expression of his or her faith and trust in God. The participants may want to begin by reflecting on these questions:

- What do you believe about God?
- When in your experience have you turned to God for help, protection, or strength?
- What gives you confidence that God is with you?

Bring the group together. Conclude the activity by inviting the group members to pray together Psalm 46 or read aloud to them one of the Psalm prayers found on page 82 of this guide.

Engaging the Word (lectio divina, 45 minutes)

Use the steps outlined for leading group *lectio divina* to guide the group through contemplation of **Psalm 23**. (See pages 12–13, leader's guide.)

As a concluding step, invite the group to say together Psalm 23.

Closing (5 minutes)

Ask each person to reflect in silence and consider these questions:

- How has your faith been influenced by what God has done in the past? by what God promises for the future?
- In what ways does your faith affect the way you live?
- What would it mean, this coming week, to live your daily life always trusting God?

Invite the group members to sing together a hymn of faith.

Invite the group to say responsively Psalm 121:1-2 or read aloud one of the Psalm prayers found on pages 83–84 of this guide.

> I lift up my eyes to the hills—
>   from where will my help come?
> My help comes from the LORD,
>   who made heaven and earth.

Conclude with a benediction: **May the Lord of heaven and earth be with you.**

Extinguish the candle.

Notes on Psalm 46

"God is our refuge and strength, a very present help in trouble." The word *refuge* is closer in meaning to "sanctuary"; God is a safe house, where we are protected. The word *present* also means "proven." In the past, God has helped God's people. We trust that God will continue to help us in the present. Verses 1-3 are a statement of faith: Because we trust in God—and because God is trustworthy—we will not fear. No matter what happens, we turn to God with confidence.

The scenes of trouble in verses 2-3—"the earth changes," "the mountains shake," "the waters roar and foam"—combined with God's commandment to be still (v. 10) bring to mind both the beginning and the end of time. In the beginning was chaos, ordered by the voice of God (Gen. 1:1-5). At the end, waters of life and abundance flow from the throne of God; God's home is among the people (Rev. 21:1-5; 22:1-5); and God establishes eternal peace (Isa. 65:17-25). God stands at the boundaries—the beginning and the end—of human life.

Psalm 46 celebrates God's power over both the natural world and the human community. Though the mountains shake, God will not be moved. Though the nations are in an uproar, God silences them with a word: "Be still."

"Know that I am God!" The psalm clearly affirms that the God who stands at the beginning and the end of time, the God who is Lord of heaven and earth, is also the God who is with us here and now, our refuge and strength in every trouble.

Permission is granted to make one copy for each participant.

Honest to God

The life of prayer, like life itself, is not always happy and peaceful. Into prayer we take our anxieties, loneliness, and discouragement along with our joy, awe, and celebration. *In order to deepen any intimate relationship, we must be honest about our feelings.* Relating to the God of the universe is no different. In fact, God knows us better than we know ourselves and always desires "truth in the inward being" (Ps. 51:6).

The book of Psalms demonstrates such honest prayer. It contains songs of praise and prayers of lament, hymns celebrating God's steadfast love, and prayers for vindication against enemies. The psalmists recall God's faithful love and extol the marvels of the created order. As we read, we share the psalmists' loneliness, sickness, grief, and dread. We experience with them the ups and downs of their genuine spiritual journeys.

Perhaps no other book in the Bible has been read and meditated on as much as the book of Psalms. In most monasteries, the Psalms are recited from morning until night. Through prayerful repetition, the Psalms reach deeper and deeper into our hearts. *When we "pray the psalms," we find new dimensions in our relationship with God.* The Psalms are a sanctuary of prayer to which we may daily retreat and find crucial nourishment for our hearts.

Key Verse: Your word is a lamp to my feet
and a light to my path (Psalm 119:105).

About the Psalter

If you are not Anglican or Episcopalian, you may not be familiar with the riches to be found in The Book of Common Prayer (BCP). *We include two articles from the* BCP: *"About the Psalter" and "A Guide for Reading the Psalms in One Month." The guide may be reproduced and distributed to participants during the first meeting of the* Entering the Psalms *study.*

Concerning the Psalter

The Psalter is a body of liturgical poetry. It is designed for vocal, congregational use, whether by singing or reading. There are several traditional methods of psalmody. The exclusive use of a single method makes the recitation of the Psalter needlessly monotonous. The traditional methods, each of which can be elaborate or simple, are the following:

Direct recitation denotes the reading or chanting of a whole psalm, or portion of a psalm, in unison. It is particularly appropriate for the psalm verses suggested in the lectionary for use between the Lessons at the Eucharist, when the verses are recited rather than sung, and may often be found a satisfactory method of chanting them.

Antiphonal recitation is the verse-by-verse alternation between groups of singers or readers; *e.g.*, between choir and congregation, or between one side of the congregation and the other. The alternate recitation concludes either with the Gloria Patri, or with a refrain (called the antiphon) recited in unison. This is probably the most satisfying method for reciting the psalms in the Daily Office.

Responsorial recitation is the name given to a method of psalmody in which the verses of a psalm are sung by a solo voice, with the choir and congregation singing a refrain after each verse or group of verses. This was the traditional method of singing the Venite, and the restoration of Invitatory Antiphons for Venite makes possible a recovery of this form of sacred song in the Daily Office. It was also a traditional manner of chanting the psalms between the Lessons at the Eucharist, and it is increasingly favored by modern composers.

Responsive recitation is the method which has been most frequently used in Episcopal churches, the minister alternating with the congregation, verse by verse.

The version of the Psalms which follows is set out in lines of poetry. The lines correspond to Hebrew versification, which is not based on meter or rhyme, but on parallelism of clauses, a symmetry of form and sense. The parallelism can take the form of similarity (The waters have lifted up, O Lord / the waters have lifted up their voice; / the waters have lifted up the pounding waves. *Psalm 93:4*), or of contrast (The Lord knows the ways of the righteous; / but the way of the wicked is doomed. *Psalm 1:6*), or of logical expansion (Our eyes look to the Lord our God, / until he show us his mercy. *Psalm 123:3*).

The most common verse is a couplet, but triplets are very frequent, and quatrains are not unknown; although quatrains are usually distributed over two verses.

· · ·

Three terms are used in the Psalms with reference to God: *Elohim* ("God"), *Adonai* ("Lord") and the personal name *YHWH*. The "Four-letter Name" (Tetragrammaton) is probably to be vocalized Yahweh; but this is by no means certain, because from very ancient times it has been considered too sacred to be pronounced; and, whenever it occurred, *Adonai* was substituted for it. In the oldest manuscripts, the Divine Name was written in antique and obsolete letters; in more recent manuscripts and in printed Bibles, after the invention of vowel points, the Name was provided with the vowels of the word *Adonai*. This produced a hybrid form which has been transliterated "Jehovah."

The Hebrew reverence and reticence with regard to the Name of God has been carried over into the classical English versions, the Prayer Book Psalter and the King James Old Testament, where it is regularly rendered "Lord." In order to distinguish it, however, from "Lord" as a translation of *Adonai, YHWH* is represented in capital and small capital letters: LORD.

From time to time, the Hebrew text has *Adonai* and *YHWH* in conjunction. Then, the Hebrew custom is to substitute *Elohim* for *YHWH*, and our English tradition follows suit, rendering the combined title as "Lord God."

In two passages (*Psalm 68:4* and *Psalm 83:18*) the context requires that the Divine Name be spelled out, and it appears as YAHWEH. A similar construction occurs in the Canticle, "The Song of Moses."

The ancient praise-shout, "Hallelujah," has been restored, in place of its English equivalent, "Praise the Lord." The Hebrew form has been used, rather than the Latin form "Alleluia," as being more appropriate to this context; but also to regain for our liturgy a form of the word that is familiar from its use in many well-known anthems. The word may, if desired, be omitted during the season of Lent.

(From *The Book of Common Prayer*, pages 582–84)

A Guide for Reading the Psalms in One Month

First Day: Morning Prayer
Psalms 1–5

First Day: Evening Prayer
Psalms 6–8

Second Day: Morning Prayer
Psalms 9–11

Second Day: Evening Prayer
Psalms 12–14

Third Day: Morning Prayer
Psalms 15–17

Third Day: Evening Prayer
Psalm 18

Fourth Day: Morning Prayer
Psalms 19–21

Fourth Day: Evening Prayer
Psalms 22–23

Fifth Day: Morning Prayer
Psalm 24–26

Fifth Day: Evening Prayer
Psalms 27–29

Sixth Day: Morning Prayer
Psalms 30–31

Sixth Day: Evening Prayer
Psalms 32–34

Seventh Day: Morning Prayer
Psalms 35–36

Seventh Day: Evening Prayer
Psalm 37

Eighth Day: Morning Prayer
Psalms 38–40

Eighth Day: Evening Prayer
Psalms 41–43

Ninth Day: Morning Prayer
Psalms 44–46

Ninth Day: Evening Prayer
Psalms 47–49

Tenth Day: Morning Prayer
Psalms 50–52

Tenth Day: Evening Prayer
Psalms 53–55

Eleventh Day: Morning Prayer
Psalms 56–58

Eleventh Day: Evening Prayer
Psalms 59–61

Twelfth Day: Morning Prayer
Psalms 62–64

Twelfth Day: Evening Prayer
Psalms 65–67

Thirteenth Day: Morning Prayer
Psalm 68

Thirteenth Day: Evening Prayer
Psalms 69–70

Fourteenth Day: Morning Prayer
Psalms 71–72

Fourteenth Day: Evening Prayer
Psalms 73–74

Fifteenth Day: Morning Prayer
Psalms 75–77

Fifteenth Day: Evening Prayer
Psalm 78

Sixteenth Day: Morning Prayer
Psalms 79–81

Sixteenth Day: Evening Prayer
Psalms 82–85

Seventeenth Day: Morning Prayer
Psalms 86–88

Seventeenth Day: Evening Prayer
Psalm 89

Eighteenth Day: Morning Prayer
Psalms 90–92

Eighteenth Day: Evening Prayer
Psalms 93–94

Nineteenth Day: Morning Prayer
Psalms 95–97

Nineteenth Day: Evening Prayer
Psalms 98–101

Twentieth Day: Morning Prayer
Psalms 102–103

Twentieth Day: Evening Prayer
Psalm 104

Twenty-first Day: Morning Prayer
Psalm 105

Twenty-first Day: Evening Prayer
Psalm 106

Twenty-second Day: Morning Prayer
Psalm 107

Twenty-second Day: Evening Prayer
Psalms 108–109

Twenty-third Day: Morning Prayer
Psalms 110–113

Twenty-third Day: Evening Prayer
Psalms 114–115

Twenty-fourth Day: Morning Prayer
Psalms 116–118

Twenty-fourth Day: Evening Prayer
Psalm 119:1-32

Twenty-fifth Day: Morning Prayer
Psalm 119:33-72

Twenty-fifth Day: Evening Prayer
Psalm 119:73-104

Twenty-sixth Day: Morning Prayer
Psalm 119:105-144

Twenty-sixth Day: Evening Prayer
Psalm 119:145-176

Twenty-seventh Day: Morning Prayer
Psalms 120–125

Twenty-seventh Day: Evening Prayer
Psalms 126–131

Twenty-eighth Day: Morning Prayer
Psalms 132–135

Twenty-eighth Day: Evening Prayer
Psalms 136–138

Twenty-ninth Day: Morning Prayer
Psalms 139-140

Twenty-ninth Day: Evening Prayer
Psalms 141–143

Thirtieth Day: Morning Prayer
Psalms 144–146

Thirtieth Day: Evening Prayer
Psalms 147–150

(From The Book of Common Prayer, pages 585–88)

Psalm Prayers

Session 1

Psalm Prayer (Ps. 147 or General Use)

O God of generous love and abundant mercy,
    how good it is to sing your praises.
Your steadfast love has been known in all the generations;
    and we celebrate that love this day.
As we place our hope in you,
    may we be your faithful servants. **Amen.**

Ps. 147; adapt. by Jerry Oakland
Adapt. © 2006 Upper Room Books

Psalm Prayer (Ps. 147 or General Use)

We praise you, O great and glorious God.
We thank you that you take pleasure in your creation
    and that you are at work healing and restoring your people.
May our songs of love and praise be a faithful witness to you. **Amen.**

Ps. 147; adapt. by Judy Holloway
Adapt. © 2006 Upper Room Books

Psalm Prayer (Ps. 147 or General Use)

O God, you tend to the stars, the grass,
    the animals and birds with gentle care.
You provide food and drink for all your creatures.
In the same way, you lift the fallen,
    heal the sick and brokenhearted,
    establish peace where there is conflict.
We glorify your name and worship you with thanks and praise. **Amen.**

Ps. 147; adapt. by Ginger Howl
Adapt. © 2006 Upper Room Books

Psalm Prayer (Ps. 147 or General Use)

Our hands clap, our feet dance, and our voices shout:

Amen! Hallelujah!

You are our sovereign, you are exalted!

Hallelujah! Amen!

Ps. 147; adapt. by Elise S. Eslinger
Adapt. © 2006 Upper Room Books

Session 2

Psalm Prayer (Ps. 130)

Waiting for you, O God . . .
>   you will come, as sure as the morning,
>   bringing hope, forgiveness,
>   and redemption. **Amen.**

Ps. 130; adapt. by Larry Peacock
Adapt. © 2006 Upper Room Books

Session 3

Psalm Prayer (Ps. 122)

O God of the holy places, of the sacred and the profane,
    guide our steps to you and hear our prayers for your people.
May your goodness bring the blessing of peace
    throughout the earth, in every land. **Amen.**

Ps. 122; adapt. by Jerry Oakland
Adapt. © 2006 Upper Room Books

Psalm Prayer (Ps. 122)

Holy God, we pray with your people throughout the ages—
    Let there be peace in Jerusalem.
And not only Jerusalem, but may peace come to every great city,
    every hamlet, every home in the universe
    that you created and called "very good." **Amen.**

Ps. 122; adapt. by Ginger Howl
Adapt. © 2006 Upper Room Books

Psalm Prayer (Ps. 122)

O God of Peace,
    it is a delight to gather with your people in your holy presence.
Fill us with your desire for peace
    so that we may speak and act for harmony in our homes,
    our communities, and your world. **Amen.**

Ps. 122; adapt. by Jo Hoover
Adapt. © 2006 Upper Room Books

Psalm Prayer (Ps. 100)

Holy God, with people of all lands we joyfully serve you
    and sing praises in your presence.
Your mercy and faithfulness are our guiding lights.
    Praise be to you, O God. **Amen.**

Ps. 100; adapt. by Ginger Howl
Adapt. © 2006 Upper Room Books

Psalm Prayer (Ps. 100)

Shepherding God, we join with all creation
    in bringing you joyful thanks and glad songs of praise,
    for your love endures and your faithfulness lasts forever. **Amen.**

Ps. 100; adapt. by Larry Peacock
Adapt. © 2006 Upper Room Books

Psalm Prayer (Ps. 100)

O Everlasting Love, what joy to be in your presence.
How wonderful to know that you created us.
How we marvel that you have made us your own.
Keep us mindful of your faithfulness.
Enfold us in your enduring love forever. **Amen.**

Ps. 100; adapt. by Jo Hoover
Adapt. © 2006 Upper Room Books

Session 6

Psalm Prayer (Ps. 16)

Indeed, faithful God, you have shown us the path of life
    and given us a heritage of unspeakable richness.
You call us now into joyful trust of the future you bring.
We abide in you. **Amen.**

Ps. 16; adapt. by Elise S. Eslinger
Adapt. © 2006 Upper Room Books

Psalm Prayer (Ps. 46)

Though the world shakes us and life overwhelms us,
    you are our help, our strength.
You still our hearts and turn us
    and the whole earth toward peace.
You are our refuge, O God. **Amen.**

Ps. 46; adapt. by Larry Peacock
Adapt. © 2006 Upper Room Books

Psalm Prayer (Ps. 46)

God of refuge, we come to you,
    placing our trust in you
    and seeking your protection.
In your tenderness and mercy you gather us close,
    sustaining us in the midst of trial
    and encouraging us in the midst of terror.
Bless us always in the shelter of your abiding grace. **Amen.**

Ps. 46; adapt. by Jerry Oakland
Adapt. © 2006 Upper Room Books

Psalm Prayer (Ps. 121)

Not from the hills but from you, O God,
    my help, my shield, my shelter.
Keep us from evil and guard all our journeys. **Amen.**

Ps. 121; adapt. by Larry Peacock
Adapt. © 2006 Upper Room Books

Psalm Prayer (Ps. 121)

You have been our help forever and ever,
    guarding, watching, and protecting.
Through the day and all during the night, Loving Creator,
    you are with us. **Amen.**

Ps. 121; adapt. by Larry Peacock
Adapt. © 2006 Upper Room Books

Psalm Prayer (Ps. 121)

O God, ever wakeful, ever vigilant,
    your protection and loving care are always with us.
Even in times when evil seems rampant,
    in times of natural disaster,
    in times of anxiety or grief,
    you guard our going out and our coming in.
Through Jesus Christ we know your grace is sufficient. **Amen.**

Ps. 121; adapt. by Ginger Howl
Adapt. © 2006 Upper Room Books

Psalm Prayer (Ps. 121)

O Protector God, ever close and attentive:
    you know each step we take and each word we utter.
We rest our souls in you and have nothing to fear.
Thank you for this unmerited blessing. **Amen.**

Ps. 121; adapt. by Jerry Oakland
Adapt. © 2006 Upper Room Books

Psalm Prayer (Ps. 121)

Today, O God, I rest in the hope of your love and protection,
    for my help comes from you.
You will not let my foot slip. You watch over me day and night.
You keep me in the safety of your eternal love
    now and forevermore. **Amen.**

Ps. 121; adapt. by Sheri Daylong
Adapt. © 2006 Upper Room Books

What Is Spiritual Formation?

HUMAN BEINGS ARE creatures of the future. Unlike other inhabitants of creation whose lives are fixed within the boundaries of genetics and instinct, human existence is open-ended, laced with mystery, like moist clay in a potter's hand. We are works in progress, shaped by the constant rhythms of nature and the unexpected turns of history. Sometimes elated and sometimes burdened by our unfinished condition, we live our days conscious that "what we will be has not yet been made known" (1 John 3:2). A sense of our true identity is always just beyond our grasp, always awaiting us, it seems, just around the next bend in the road.

As nature and history interact with a human existence that is incomplete, pliable, and rich with significant potential, personal formation occurs. *Human beings are formed by the sculpting of will, intellect, and emotion into a distinct way of being in the world.* Such formation of personal character will assume a wide range of expression depending on our location geographically, socially, economically, and culturally. Family values, social conventions, cultural assumptions, the great turning points of an epoch, the painful secrets of a heart—these and many other factors combine to form or deform the direction, depth, and boundaries of our lives. Formation is therefore a fundamental characteristic of human life. It is happening whether or not we are aware of it, and its effect may as often inhibit as promote the development of healthy, fulfilled humanity.

For people of biblical faith, nature and history of themselves are not the final sources of personal formation. Rather, they are means through which the God who formed all things molds human beings into the contours of their truest destiny: the unfettered praise of God (see Isaiah 43:21). To be shaped by God's gracious design is a particular expression of personal formation—spiritual formation. Irenaeus, third-century bishop of Lyons, echoed this ancient biblical theme when he observed that *"the glory of God is the human being fully alive."* The God known in scripture is a God who continuously forms something out of nothing—earth and heaven, creatures great and small, a people who call upon God's name, the "inmost being" (Ps. 139:13) of every human life. Yet the majestic sweep of God's formational activity never eclipses the intimacy God desires and seeks with us. Having carefully and lovingly formed each of us in the womb, God knows us by name and will not forget us (see Isaiah 43:1; 44:21, 24). In the biblical perspective, to be a person means to exist in a relationship of ongoing spiritual formation with the God whose interest in us extends to the very roots of our being.

For Christians, the pattern and fulfillment of God's work of spiritual formation converge in a single figure—Jesus Christ. Jesus is the human being fully alive, fully open to God's work in the world. Simultaneously, Jesus is God's work fully alive, fully embodied in the world. For all who are heavily burdened and wearied by the torments of the world, for all who long to dwell in the house of the Lord, Jesus is the level way, the whole truth, and the radiant life. Christians are placed daily before the greatest of all choices: *to be conformed to the luminous image of Jesus Christ* through the gracious assistance of God the Holy Spirit or to be conformed to the ravaged image of the world through the deceitful encouragement of the "cosmic powers of this present darkness " (Eph. 6:12).

Spiritual formation in the Christian tradition, then, is a lifelong process through which our new humanity, hidden with Jesus Christ in God, becomes ever more visible and effective through the leading of the Holy Spirit. *Spiritual formation at its best has been understood to be at once fully divine and fully human—that is, initiated by God and manifest in both vital communities of faith and in the lives of individual disciples.* We see this theme carried through the history of the church, from Paul's introduction of formation in Jesus Christ as the central work of Christian life (Galatians 4:19) to early formational writings such as the Didache (second century); to the formative intent of monastic rules; to the shaping purpose of Protestant manuals of piety; to the affirmation of lay formation in the documents of Vatican II; and finally to the current search for practices that open us to God.

Our unfinished character leads us to acknowledge that *"what we will be has not yet been revealed."* Yet Christians, looking at Jesus Christ, can add with confident hope that "we will be like him" (1 John 3:2). This hope originates in the hidden dimensions of baptism. Baptism unites us with the full sweep of Jesus' life and death, resurrection, and ascension in glory to the eternal communion of love enjoyed by our triune God. In baptism, motifs of cleansing from the stain of sin coexist with images of death and rebirth to signal the radically new life we enter through this spiritual birth canal (John 3:1-6).

At the center of this rebirth from above is the Paschal mystery—*the pattern of self-relinquishment and loving availability Jesus freely manifested in his ministry and in his final journey* to Jerusalem and Golgotha. This is the mysterious pattern of God's work in the world, the pattern of loss that brings gain, willing sacrifice that yields abundance, self-forgetfulness that creates a space for the remembering God. It is the pattern that steers our course from bondage to freedom—from the ways of the old Adam, who turned and hid from the One who so lovingly formed him, *to the freedom of the new Adam*, Jesus Christ, who lives with God in unbroken intimacy.

This unfolding of baptismal grace in daily life, this passing from bondage to freedom, is spiritual formation. Because *spiritual formation draws us into the fullness of life in Jesus Christ*, it shares the qualities of Jesus Christ. Thus, spiritual formation is eminently personal yet inherently corporate: *It erases nothing of our unique humanity but transposes it into a larger reality*—the mystical body of Jesus Christ in and through which we are, as the Episcopal Book of Common Prayer notes, "very members incorporate" of one another. Spiritual formation is also fully human, reflecting our own decisions, commitments, disciplines, and actions. At the same time, *spiritual formation is wholly divine, an activity initiated by God and completed by God*, in which we have been generously embraced for the sake of the world.

THE HOLY SPIRIT'S LEADING

The sweeping movement of grace by which the world was created and is sustained is orchestrated by God the Holy Spirit. In God's sovereign freedom, the Holy Spirit stirs where the Spirit chooses. Remarkably, *the Spirit has selected human life as a privileged place of redemptive activity.* In the day-to-day rhythms of our life, the Holy Spirit comes to us with gentle persistence, inviting us to join the wondrous dance of life with God. In this holy dance the Spirit always takes the lead, a partner both sensitive and sure. ***"The spiritual life is the life of God's Spirit in us,"*** notes spiritual writer Marjorie Thompson, "the living interaction between our spirit and the Holy Spirit through which we mature into the full stature of Christ and become more surrendered to the work of the Spirit within and around us."

There are settings and disciplines that prepare us to recognize and respond to the Holy Spirit's invitation. The church, the body of Jesus Christ visible and tangible in the world, as rich with promise as it is with paradox—is the principal context in which to sharpen our spiritual senses. The mere fact of gathering with others on the Lord's Day reminds us that the Holy Spirit continuously draws together what evil strives to scatter. In congregational worship, we hear God's word to us; recall how lavishly God loves us; see this love enacted in baptism; taste its sweetness and its wonder in the Lord's Supper; and take stock of our response to it in confession, hymn, and corporate prayer. Small groups given to prayer, study, or outreach also offer places to increase our awareness of the Holy Spirit's leading. In the company of faithful seekers, another person's moment of vulnerability, a truth spoken in love or a story told in trust can awaken insight into ways the Holy Spirit is also present with us. Family life, which Martin Luther placed ahead of the monastery as the true school of charity, provides many opportunities to learn the art of self-forgetfulness. ***Time spent with the poor and needy instructs us in our own poverty***, prepares us to receive more than we bestow from those who often seem so distressingly different, and gives the Spirit occasion to teach us the extent of our common humanity.

Personal spiritual practices also prime us to be responsive to the Holy Spirit's approach. The meditative reading of scripture encouraged in this Bible enables us to become at home in God's word. As this occurs, we develop a growing familiarity with the Holy Spirit who fashioned and continues to dwell in holy writ. According to twelfth-century Cistercian abbot Peter of Celle, such reading is nothing less than "the soul's food, light, lamp, refuge, consolation, and the spice of every spiritual savor." ***Prayer, that royal road to deepening intimacy with God, will inevitably acquaint us with the guiding grace of the Spirit.*** It is in the Spirit that we pray and through the Spirit that the inarticulate yearnings of our heart receive coherent expression before God (see Rom. 8:27). Various "spiritual fitness" exercises, including abstaining from self-destructive activities and attitudes, allocating personal resources in a godly manner, and following simple rules of life help to ***remind us that God is the center of each day***. Such exercises produce stamina for continued acceptance of the Holy Spirit's invitation to "come and follow."

Following the leading of the Holy Spirit builds in us a growing capacity for extraordinary witness to God's kingdom, such as extending forgiveness where there has been genuine injury. It also reinforces in us the knowledge that *our new humanity in Jesus Christ is the work of the Spirit and not our own achievement.* In our human weakness, we need the strength and sustenance of the Holy Spirit to maintain the Godward direction of our life. Such assistance is clearly promised by Jesus: "When the Spirit of truth comes, he will guide you into all the truth" (John 16:13). This truth is what the author of Ephesians calls "the full stature of Christ" (Eph. 4:13). The measure of this truth is nothing other than love. *Love is the first gift of the Spirit and the final test of our freedom in Jesus Christ* (see 1 Cor. 13; Gal. 5:22; Col. 1:8). All other marks of our new humanity—joy, peace, patience, kindness, generosity, faithfulness, self-control—are manifestations of this love, a love that binds us to Jesus Christ in the unity of the Holy Spirit for the sake of the world God loves so much. "If we live by the Spirit, let us also be guided by the Spirit" (Gal. 5:25).

IN THE WORLD

In a life increasingly given to the guidance of the Holy Spirit, our new humanity in Jesus Christ gradually becomes more visible and effective in the world. Far from removing us from the messiness of the world, *spiritual formation plunges us into the middle of the world's rage and suffering.* It was to this place of pain and bewilderment that Jesus Christ was sent as the visible image of the invisible God (see John 14:9; Col. 1:15). It was to this place of bitterness and infirmity that Jesus Christ was sent, not to condemn but to save (see John 3:17). Those who are being formed in his image take the same path. Love, the full measure of Christian maturity, impels us with kindly urgency in this direction. *Love desires to be seen, known and received, for by these actions it grows wider and deeper.* Through us love is extended to the furthest recesses of human sorrow and need. Thus, God's love for the world—in us because we are in Jesus Christ—becomes a sign of hope and a source of transformation in the world.

"No one is richer, no one more powerful, no one more free," observed Thomas à Kempis, "than *the person who can give his whole life to God and freely serve others with deep humility and love.*" To embody in thought, word, and deed the love of God made known in our Lord Jesus Christ is the signal mark of faithful discipleship, the inexhaustible strength of vital congregations, and the ultimate goal of spiritual formation.

—John Mogabgab

Meeting God in

Scripture

IN EVERY ERA, in myriad places and in all kinds of circumstances, people have testified that the Bible speaks powerfully—that the Word of God can and does change lives. But perhaps you feel that your own experience with reading the Bible pales in significance when compared to such a standard. You feel like the woman who confessed, *"Surely there has to be a way to get more out of my Bible reading!"* Your times with the Bible yield much of value and interest—but transformation? That is another matter. You learn facts—places and names—but have yet to hear God's voice. As much as you value the insights gained, you long to meet God.

When you read and study scripture *it is possible to grow beyond an intellectual knowledge of the Bible to the transformation of your heart.* The Bible can become "a lamp to [your] feet and a light for [your] path" (Ps. 119:105). You can go to the heart of the matter and meet the Author. The eighteenth-century bishop Tikhon of Zodonsk articulated well what can happen: "Whenever you read the Gospel," he wrote, "Christ Himself is speaking to you. And while you read, you are praying and talking to Him." Reading and studying the Bible can become more fulfilling than anything you have previously experienced.

But how? Providentially we are heirs to several helpful approaches. The great spiritual writers of the past have given us a legacy that engages mind and heart, intellect and will. They have suggested ways that help us derive life from the text and so become agents of life for others.

DIVINE READING

In the history of Christian spirituality, the oldest and best-known approach to Bible reading is called "spiritual reading" or "divine reading" (the Latin is *lectio divina*). The practice dates back to at least the fourth century, but the idea behind it is even more ancient. Spiritual reading entails a fourfold approach:

First, read slowly. Choose a relatively short passage of a biblical book (no more than several paragraphs or a short chapter), and read meditatively, prayerfully. In this phase you are a seeker looking for the "word within the Word." **Watch for a key phrase or word that jumps out at you** or promises to have special meaning for you. Concern yourself not so much with the amount you are reading as the depth with which you read. It is better to dwell profoundly on one word or phrase than to skim the surface of several chapters. **Read with your own life and choices in view,** recalling the biblical injunction that God's word is "useful for teaching, for reproof, for correction, and for training in righteousness" (2 Tim. 3:16).

Second, meditate. Christian meditation is not stream of consciousness or free association, nor is it Eastern transcendental meditation. Rather, **it is letting a special word or phrase that you discovered in the first phase of reading sink into your heart.** It is what the biblical writers had in mind when they spoke of "meditating" on the Book of the Law "day and night" (Josh. 1:8; Ps. 1:2). For example, when you are reading Psalm 23, perhaps you linger at the phrase, "The LORD is my shepherd." For reasons that may not be immediately apparent, the word *my* stands out. You are struck by the idea that God can be—and wants to be—your shepherd. In this second phase of spiritual reading, stay with that thought. Use whatever study skills and related materials that are available to you to enrich your reflection. **Bring mind, will, and emotions to the enterprise.** This meditative stage is comparable to walking around a great statue, viewing it from multiple vantage points. You are like Mary, Jesus' mother, who heard of the angel's announcement and "treasured up" and "pondered" what she had heard (Luke 2:19).

Third, pray the text. You have listened; now you respond—that is, **you form a prayer that expresses your response to the idea.** You "pray it back to God." You are, in effect, engaging

God in dialogue. In the case of "The LORD is my shepherd," your response could easily be a prayer of gratitude. It might be a prolonged recollection of all of the ways that God has been present with you over the years, shepherding you through life. This phase of divine reading is in reality not separate from the other aspects but flows through all of them, so that *you are continually converting the text into a prayer,* a prayer formed by God's revealed will. What you have read is woven through what you tell God. You thereby acknowledge that God's Word "shall not return . . . empty, but it shall accomplish that which [God desires]" (Isa. 55:11).

Fourth, contemplate. That is, rest. In divine reading you eventually arrive at the place where you no longer work on the text but allow it to work itself into you. *You let it soak into your deepest being.* You do not strain for additional insights; you simply savor an encounter—with God's truth and God's own self. You enjoy the rest that Jesus promised those who come to him (see Matthew 11:28). Quietly, when ready, move toward the moment in which you *ask God to show you how to live out what you have experienced.*

Spiritual reading enables God to "speak and show" in ways that transform the written word into a living Word—just for you. Then, having "taste[d] and see[n] that the LORD is good" (Ps. 34:8), *you move outward in daily living to become a blessing to others.*

IGNATIAN READING

Attributed to Ignatius of Loyola (1491–1556) and articulated in his "Spiritual Exercises," the Ignatian method of reading the Bible likewise invites us to enter actively and fully into the text. *It encourages detachment from either ego-driven success or fear-motivated anxiety,* leaving the soul free to obey God's stirrings.

Generally, Ignatian reading works best with narrative material in which actual characters lived a story of faith. The idea is to *place yourself into the text as a careful observer*—a "fly on the wall," if you will. Ignatius commended the use of the five senses in such meditation. You taste, hear, see, smell, and feel your way through the passage. Occasionally you become one of the characters, seeing the story unfold from his or her viewpoint. Most of all, the aim is to help you *perceive the narrative from the viewpoint of Jesus so that you may more fully participate in his mind, heart, and work.*

For the sake of practice, you might like to concentrate on John 18:1-11 and spend five days reading it. Each day, imagine yourself as a different one of the characters: Judas, a soldier, Peter, the high priest's servant, or Jesus. As you enter vicariously into the position of each character, *ask God to teach you how to live in greater fidelity and obedience*—which is the ultimate aim of the Ignatian method of reading scripture and of Ignatian spirituality in general.

FRANCISCAN READING

While not a direct by-product of the teachings of Francis of Assisi, Franciscan reading exhibits primary qualities of Franciscan spirituality, such as action, spontaneity, love, praise, beauty, and delight in creation. Like Ignatian reflection, Franciscan reading involves the mental process of entering personally into the text. But this method is more fluid, *allowing the encounter with God to incorporate daily activities and experiences.*

For example, turn in your Bible to Isaiah 53 and read through this chapter. To help you enter into its message and reflect on Jesus' sacrificial death on the cross, the Franciscan method would invite you to take actions such as these: If you have a model of a cross with Jesus on it, you might hold it in your hand, gazing at the details of the Lord's crucified body. You might sing a hymn such as "O Sacred Head, Now Wounded" or "The Old Rugged Cross." You might look through today's newspaper and identify places in the world where people are suffering. You might write a poem or paint a picture to capture what you are thinking and feeling. In the Franciscan spirit, you would express your emotions through an activity. You would be encouraged to "feel" something of what Jesus experienced on your behalf. You would saturate the entire experience with prayer, *asking God to make you an instrument of peace* in the lives of those who suffer.

These methods do not exhaust our options for formative reading. You might use the fruit of the Spirit described in Galatians 5:22–23 as a lens through which you read, asking yourself how a particular passage might deepen love, joy, peace, patience, kindness, goodness, gentleness, faithfulness, and self-control in your life. You might use the Fivefold Question (What does this passage say about God's nature? What does it say about human nature? What does it say about how God relates to people? What does it suggest about how I might pray? What does it suggest about how I might act?).

Whatever method you use at any given time, adopt an underlying attitude of openness to seeking truth. We pray for a "scriptural mind" that is obedient, faithful to the historic Christian tradition, Christ-centered and personal. *We must desire to find truth and be willing to apply it to our own lives* and our relationships with others. Apart from such foundational commitments, any method becomes mere technique. With them, any of the methods of reading scripture can become a true means of grace.

—J. STEVEN HARPER

Praying the

Scriptures

A LONGTIME MEMBER of a well-established Protestant church recounted a turning point in her spiritual life: She discovered that the Bible could be prayed as well as read. She had read, studied, and reflected on the Bible for many years, yet the notion of "praying the scriptures" seemed quite foreign when a friend first suggested it. Nonetheless, as soon as she began to practice praying the scriptures, it made complete sense. For the first time in her adult life, the Bible truly came alive. She experienced the Word of God as "living and active" (Heb. 4:12), a means through which God searched, invited, challenged, and comforted her. It seemed so natural that she felt as if she had spiritually "come home."

To pray the scriptures means to allow the words of the sacred text to form our prayer—either directly or indirectly. Prayer entails heart-to-heart communication with God that moves in both directions. God speaks, we listen and respond; we speak, God listens and responds.

To pray the scriptures requires first of all that we approach the Word in a spirit of prayer. ***We acknowledge that we are seeking the living, active presence of God in and through God's Word.*** We bring ourselves consciously into the divine presence and affirm the reality of this presence even if we cannot feel it. Whatever we read and reflect on in the Word is part of our ongoing dialogue with God.

From this basic stance, we may take any number of approaches to praying the scriptures. One of the most central and ancient practices of Christian prayer is called *lectio divina,* or spiritual reading. In *lectio divina,* we begin by reading and savoring a short passage of scripture. ***Our inner posture is one of a listening heart filled with an unhurried expectation that God has a message to convey*** especially suited to our condition and circumstance. We read and ruminate with the ears of our heart open, alert to connections the Spirit may reveal between the passage and our life situation. We ask, ***"What are you saying to me today, Lord?*** What am I to hear in this story, parable, prophecy?" Listening in this way requires an attitude of patient receptivity in which we let go of our own agendas and open ourselves to God's shaping purpose.

LECTIO DIVINA

Once we have heard a word that we know is meant for our ears, we are naturally drawn to prayer. ***From listening we move to speaking***—perhaps in anguish, confession, or sorrow; perhaps in joy, praise, thanksgiving, or adoration; perhaps in anger, confusion, or hurt; perhaps in quiet confidence, trust, or surrender. Finally, after pouring out our heart to God, we come to rest simply and deeply in that wonderful, loving presence of God. Reading, reflecting, responding, and resting—this is the basic rhythm of a venerable and often-used approach to scripture called *lectio divina.*

Perhaps an example will help to bring this rhythm alive in your imagination. Recently I read in Second Kings about the origins of the people called Samaritans. Samaria once belonged to the ancient kingdom of Israel. When the king of Assyria invaded, taking Israelites captive to his own land, he forcibly repopulated Samaria with people from surrounding regions who decided to worship "the god of the land." The passage reads, "They worshiped the LORD, but also served their own gods, after the manner of the nations from among whom they had been carried away" (2 Kings 17:33). I hadn't read this book in a long time, and I found myself fascinated by the history. *It would make for interesting Bible study,* I thought, *or a good sermon.* Then suddenly I heard in my mind's ear a shocking indictment: "You are a Samaritan." Recalling that I was reading for the purpose of prayer, I asked, "Are you really saying that I'm like this, God?" The answer was there in my own heart: Yes, you worship God but also the gods of this land— success, prosperity, "the American Dream." This was clearly a very uncomfortable word that God had addressed personally to me. It prompted me to reflect on all the ways I do, in fact, give my heart and allegiance to the idols of my culture. ***Recognition of that reality propelled me into prayers of confession and repentance, then prayer for the strength of*** *will to desire God above all else.* Finally, I had to confess my guilt to God and rest in the assurance of God's mercy. The whole cycle took perhaps ten or fifteen minutes.

THE IGNATIAN METHOD

Lectio divina is but one way to pray the scriptures. We can also pray the Bible by using our God-given imagination by means of an ancient method referred to as Ignatian. ***This approach invites us to enter the narrative, picturing the situation, and identifying with characters that populate the drama.*** This may eventually lead us to dialogue beyond what is given in the text, a dialogue that becomes part of our prayer. Some passages of scripture are better suited to this process than others. The Gospels are especially rich in stories that easily engage our imagination as a way to enter into prayer.

Read, for example, a story such as the tax collector and the Pharisee (see Luke 18:9-14). Picture the two men in the Temple, the Pharisee standing proudly up front, grateful not to be like the man behind him. ***Imagine what it is like to be in the shoes of someone*** who represents such high standards of righteousness according to Israelite law, who sees his life as a model of religious conduct for others. Have you ever felt like this? If so, in what kinds of situations or with what sorts of people? Then step into the shoes of the tax collector, the hated "tool of Rome." Imagine how many times you have skimmed a hefty sum for yourself from the taxes you have collected from fellow Jews for the Roman occupiers. What emotions are you experiencing—the misery of being an outcast in your own community, the self-loathing that comes from betraying your people and your integrity, the despair at your weakness of character, your desperate hope for mercy from God? With which of these two characters do you most identify? What do you have to say to God about your own experience in relation to these two characters? ***Do you see how the story and your personal engagement with it lead you into prayer?***

This approach to praying the scriptures is rich and fruitful for people who can readily exercise their God-given imagination. Perhaps you can imagine yourself as Peter, looking at the awesome catch of fish, feeling the power of the One standing before you whose eyes you dare not even look into (see Luke 5:1-11). Does this speak to your experience before God? Or perhaps you identify strongly with Martha as your sister sits idly listening to Jesus while you, in an anxious dither, rush to complete meal preparations. Do you hear Jesus' words to you as rebuke or invitation? What are you really longing for in your own heart (see Luke 10:38-42)? Maybe you are in the boat with the disciples facing a sudden and terrifying storm. You sense that the boundaries of your vision and power are limited by your fear. How do Jesus' words affect your spirit as you imagine being part of this story? What storms are you facing in your life just now? Does identification with the story make your prayer more concrete? *Is God speaking a word to you through this passage* (see Mark 4:35-41)? Or picture yourself as the woman who suffered from an issue of blood for twelve years, as you shyly thread your way through the crowd to touch the edge of Jesus' clothing. Or as Jairus, desperate for Jesus to come quickly before your daughter dies, watching Jesus turn around to find out who touched him, taking precious time to deal with the needs of someone else before he comes with you to your home (see Mark 5:21-43). Where do you connect with these powerful stories? *What insight into yourself, into God, into your relationships comes through praying the Gospels in this way?* It can be especially helpful to write down the basic outline of your imaginative encounter with the text, your insights, and any dialogue with story characters or with God that naturally occur as part of your prayer.

THE PRAYERS AND SONGS OF SCRIPTURE

There are other ways to pray scripture as well. *The Bible gives us categories for prayer, expands our language for prayer, and tutors us in speaking to God* as we hear God speak to us through the Word. The Bible contains prayers and canticles (songs) that give us words to pray and praise. Many, such as the Lord's Prayer, the Magnificat, and the Canticle of Simeon, have become part of the common prayer of church liturgy. Yet any of these may also give voice to the joys, yearnings, and struggles of our personal lives. We truly pray the Lord's Prayer when we take each phrase and make it our own, finding its truth reflected in our beliefs, needs, fears, and aspirations. Mary's Magnificat can become our own song of exultation, hope, and trust. There are times when we recognize with her that "the Mighty One has done great things for me" (Luke 1:49). We may know from experience what it means to be lifted up from lowliness, or we may see the emptiness of those who seem powerful and self-satisfied. Thus, we know that the truths spoken in Mary's words are universal precisely because they are so personal.

Sometimes *we can personalize a passage of scripture by placing our own name in it.* Some passages from the books of the Prophets lend themselves to becoming personal prayers as we make ourselves the recipients of God's Word. Take, for example, God's invitation to the abundant life in Isaiah. Insert your name in the blanks to get a feel for how to pray scripture this way:

Come, _____ who is thirsty,
    come to the waters;

and _____ who has no money,

    come, buy and eat!

_____, why spend money on what is not bread,

    and your labor on what does not satisfy?

Listen, listen to me, _____, and eat what is good . . .

    hear me, that your soul may live.

I will make an everlasting covenant with you, _____ (55:1-3, adapted).

Here **you allow yourself to receive personally the promises (or the judgments) of God and to respond from the heart.** Try this out with Isaiah 43:1-7; Jeremiah 1:4-8; or 18:1-6.

PRAYING THE BOOK OF PSALMS

The words of scripture can also become words through which we address God directly. Nowhere is this more apparent than in the book of Psalms. The book of Psalms has been called "the prayer book of the Bible" in both the Jewish and Christian traditions. It is a collection of sung prayers that has been used in corporate liturgy from the time of ancient Israel up to the present. Because the psalms range so widely in emotional expression, from the heights of adoration and praise to the depths of vengeful curses against the enemy, they have special pertinence to our prayer life. **They teach us to hide nothing from God but to bring all that is real into the only relationship that can bless the best and heal the worst in us.** Surely this is why German theologian Dietrich Bonhoeffer summoned the earthy wit of Martin Luther when he declared, "Whoever has begun to pray the Psalter seriously and regularly will soon give a vacation to other little devotional prayers and say: "'Ah, there is not the juice, the strength, the passion, the fire which I find in the Psalter' (Luther)" (*Psalms: The Prayer Book of the Bible* [Minneapolis: Augsburg Publishing House, 1970], 25).

Whether in distress, trust, anger, or delight, we find that the words of the psalms accompany us into God's presence. The Lord becomes *my* shepherd as well as the shepherd of all those who trust in him (see Psalm 23). It is I who sit down by the rivers of Babylon, lamenting my experience of exile with all who know such anguish (see Psalm 137). God is searching my heart in Psalm 139, assuring me that there is no place I can go where God's Spirit is not. Psalm 131 leads me into the peace of resting in the divine embrace like a small child with my mother. I am the poor and needy one who cries out for preservation (see Psalm 86), the one who has transgressed and needs mercy (see Psalm 51). It is I who stand looking in awe at the heavens, marveling that humans like me should count for anything in God's sight (see Psalm 8). **The psalms give** *us words to glorify, confess, hope, ask, and even curse.* In so doing, they give us permission to share our whole being with God.

Sometimes *the psalms give us words for intercession as well.* The psalm I pray may not fit *my* experience but may very well reflect the experience of another person or group. Recently, praying Psalm 107 led me into intercession for many people.

TRUST THE SPIRIT TO GUIDE YOU

There are, then, many ways to pray the scriptures. To practice any particular way, however, *we need to set aside some time each day to listen and respond to God's Word.* Even ten to fifteen minutes daily may be sufficient, although if you combine praying scripture with journaling, you will likely need twenty-five to thirty minutes. Seek a regular place for prayer as well, a place that can be free from distracting noise and interruption. Take a few moments to settle peacefully into God's presence and pray for the guidance of the Spirit. Let your body be a partner in prayer; find a comfortable posture that will keep you alert but relaxed. Then simply *trust the Spirit to guide you into prayer as your listening, your reflection, and your response are shaped by the Word of God.* Be patient with your practice. In time, rich blessings will attend you!

—MARJORIE J. THOMPSON

Meeting God in

Community

WE WERE NOT CREATED to live in isolation. No person "is an island, entire of itself," wrote the poet John Donne. While no one questions the need for periods of solitude and refreshment in our lives, faith tends to thrive most readily when shared with others. *Without the connections community affords us, we experience what someone once called "spiritual loneliness."* For we meet God not just as we sit alone in quiet corners but in and through the people with whom we live, work, and interact as we go through our daily routine.

Relationships present us with both a remarkable privilege and an awesome responsibility. Proverbs 27:17 tells us that "iron sharpens iron, and one person sharpens [and shapes] the wits of another." *As other people's lives touch ours, they help to form our faith and make us who we are.* As we touch others, we reflect God's love to them.

Relationships with other believers have extraordinary power in our lives because Jesus is present in them. *Jesus knew the importance of people in conveying God's grace and presence.* "Where two or three are gathered in my name," he said, "I am there among them" (Matt. 18:20). Within our churches, small groups, families, and friendships, we learn from one another. We find encouragement. We challenge one another to follow God more faithfully. Other Christians enable us to walk as we should when we might otherwise have strayed or wandered. *God uses relationships to form us, and relationships form us so that God can use us.*

POWER FOR GROWTH AND CHANGE

The Bible offers many examples of the formational power of relationships. The story of Ruth and Naomi demonstrates how *the presence of other believers can enable us to do what we can't do alone.* Ruth is a foreigner, a Moabite who has married Naomi's son. When Naomi's husband and her sons (including Ruth's husband) die, she grieves, saying, "The hand of the LORD has turned against me!" (Ruth 1:13). Ruth, also widowed, chooses to stay with Naomi rather than return to her own kin. Ruth speaks the words that are well-known and much-loved: "Where you go I will go; where you lodge, I will lodge; your people shall be my people, and your God my God" (Ruth 1:16). Just think of the magnitude of the change those words brought about! Something in this relationship makes Ruth willing to leave her family and country to adopt Naomi's faith. The younger woman seeks guidance from Naomi and in turn cares for her. Their loving relationship releases Naomi from the bitterness of her losses and draws Ruth into relationship with the God of Israel. Eventually Ruth becomes the ancestor of Jesus the Messiah (see Matthew 1:5).

Elijah and Elisha offer an example of the way God uses the power of relationships to build strong leaders. *God, employing Elijah as Elisha's mentor, makes a dramatic difference in the life of the younger man who is eager to serve God faithfully.* Elijah, a famous prophet, is near the end of his ministry when God tells him to seek out and anoint Elisha as his successor. Elijah throws his cloak over Elisha's shoulders as the younger man walks behind his plow and oxen, publicly calling Elisha to a new way of life. What a dramatic act! Elisha leaves his farm work to become Elijah's attendant (see 1 Kings 19:16-21), following the prophet and seeking to learn from him. He refuses to leave his mentor and asks for "a double portion" of the spirit that has made Elijah great (see 2 Kings 2:9). One man is clearly the teacher and the other the student, and, like Elijah, *Elisha acknowledges that God is at the center of his life and ministry.* Through his relationship with Elijah, he develops the courage, faith, and skills to carry on the work of the prophet as God's spokesman.

In the New Testament Mary and Elizabeth offer us yet another example of how relationships help us mature in faith. *Their relationship illustrates the value of sharing mutual insight and encouragement.* According to the Gospel of Luke, young Mary is visited by the angel Gabriel, who tells her that she will bear a son who will be the Messiah. Mary, "much perplexed by his words" (Luke 1:29), hurries to visit her older cousin Elizabeth, who is also pregnant. Though Mary has told the angel that she wants to be obedient to God's will, she is surely also confused and frightened. But after Elizabeth speaks to her, Mary breaks into a song of praise to God; her faith has been strengthened. Mary spends three months with Elizabeth, who supports her and in turn is supported in the joyful yet sacrificial work to which God has called both of them. Mary discovered, as many have, that *when we are hesitant to face what lies ahead, spending time with someone who knows us and shares our faith can help us see more clearly* and understand more deeply the issues we need to deal with. It fortifies us to move forward in faith.

SOUL FRIENDS

Throughout the history of the church, writers and leaders have echoed this message. In the twelfth century, Aelred of Rievaulx said that *Christian friendship can be "a step to raise us to the love and knowledge of God."* He also spoke of the joy of having a friend with "whom you need have no fear to confess your failings; one to whom you can unblushingly make known what progress you have made in the spiritual life; one to whom you can entrust all the secrets of your heart and before whom you can place all your plans." Teresa of Avila wrote in the sixteenth century of how *"it is a great advantage for us to be able to consult someone who knows us, so that we may learn to know ourselves."* John Wesley went so far as to declare that there is no such thing as a solitary Christian.

What these Christians from various times and places learned is that *God uses close and continuing relationships to form us into the image of Jesus.* As we share both our high moments and our low, pray for one another, help each other, and work together toward common goals, we reflect Jesus and acknowledge Jesus' presence with us.

NURTURING YOUR OWN SOUL FRIENDS

To begin to meet God in community you may want to reach out to other believers with whom you can discuss your spiritual journey. Such conversation helps you sort out what you know about yourself and about God. It may be especially valuable if this action is deliberate. Ask one or two mature individuals with whom you can exchange thoughts and prayers with confidence and assurance of confidentiality to meet with you. This practice has traditionally been called "spiritual guidance," "spiritual direction," or "spiritual friendship." This kind of conversation may also occur in the context of worship services, church school classes, and small groups. One-on-one relationships and small groups allow for a depth of interaction not possible in larger, more formal settings. They allow us to pray aloud for one another with potentially life-changing results. As Alan Jones, an essayist on Christian friendship, stated, "We cannot help but tremble on the brink of surrender, but it is our companions who give us the courage to jump."

SPEND TIME OBSERVING THE LIVES OF FAITHFUL CHRISTIANS

The New Testament tells us repeatedly that *we become like Jesus by spending time with those who are his friends.* We look at those who have led us, consider the outcome of their faith and then choose to imitate them (see Hebrews 13:7). Some find it a good discipline to think periodically about someone whose faith they admire. Consider approaching one or more such people to ask them how God has been at work in their lives. (For biblical examples of this process, see 1 Corinthians 4:6; Philippians 3:17; 1 Thessalonians 1:6; and 2 Thessalonians 3:9.)

STAY ACTIVE IN A CHURCH COMMUNITY

As happens within our immediate family circle, when we rub shoulders with others we are continually confronted with reminders of our weaknesses and brokenness. We wound others and are wounded by them. Romans 12:18 acknowledges that living with others can be difficult, urging, "If it is possible, so far as it depends on you, live peaceably with all." While imperfections abound within what Paul calls "the body of Christ," *God still uses the company of believers to grace our lives and transform the world* (see Romans 12:4-5; 1 Corinthians 12:12; Ephesians 5:30). We cannot do without our fellow believers. Let us "not [neglect] to meet together," the writer of the letter to the Hebrews urges (10:25). At their best, relationships with other believers not only shield us in difficult times but also help us to confront our imperfections. We find a place to mutually speak "the truth in love" (Eph. 4:15).

VIEW YOUR INVOLVEMENT WITH OTHER BELIEVERS AS AN OPPORTUNITY TO HELP

It is a privilege to nurture another person, to be trusted to hear another's dreams and concerns, to pray for someone. In so doing we may discover myriad ways to use the gifts that God has given us for the benefit of our family in Christ as well as for our own growth and enjoyment. As we help others, we too will be helped. As we comfort and teach and encourage, we will be comforted, taught, and encouraged in turn. As we experience community, we find our lives enriched, in turn providing us with more to give to others.

—MARY LOU REDDING

Notes

Introduction

1. The process for group *lectio* as outlined is based on Norvene Vest's book *Gathered in the Word: Praying the Scripture in Small Groups* (Nashville, TN: Upper Room Books, 1996). You may want to read Vest's book for an account of how different people respond to this way of reading scripture, but that is not necessary to the process.

About the Author

Anne Crumpler

Anne Crumpler comes from a long line of preachers, teachers, and writers; she learned theology, Bible, and English grammar over the dinner table. She also has a Bachelor of Arts in Philosophy from Chatham College and a Master of Religious Education from St. Meinrad School of Theology.

Anne has been an assistant editor in the Department of Youth Publications, the United Methodist Publishing House. She is presently a freelance writer and editor.

Anne is a contract editor for *The Upper Room* daily devotional guide and for *Devozine*. She has written Bible lessons for *Mature Years* and *Daily Bible Studies*, commentary for *The New International Lesson Annual*, articles for *Devozine* and *Alive Now*, devotions for *The Upper Room Disciplines* and *365 Meditations for Families*, sermon helps for *What Difference Would It Make?* (a program of The Upper Room), study guides for Lent and Advent offered online by The Upper Room, and lessons on the kingdom of God for volume three of *The Pastor's Bible Study*.

Anne lives in Nashville, Tennessee, with her husband, David. They have two spectacular children, Rachel and Benjamin.